DRAWING TO LEARN ANYTHING

No drawing skills required

Thank you so much for buying my little book

Paul Carney

PAUL

DRAWING TO LEARN ANYTHING

No drawing skills required

Paul Carney

First published in 2021 by: Loughborough Design Press Ltd, 12 Church Hill Road, Oxford, OX4 3SE. Copyright © 2021, Paul Carney and Loughborough Design Press.

The right of Paul Carney to be identified as the author of this book has been asserted by him in accordance with the Copyright, Designs and Patents Act, 1988.

For information on all Loughborough Design Press publications, please visit our website: www.ldpress.co.uk

Printed by Printondemand-worldwide.com, UK

The product is FSC and PEFC certified

PEFC Certified

This product is from sustainably managed forests and controlled sources

www.pefc.org

PEFC™
PEFC/16-33-415

Mixed Sources
Product group from well-managed forests, and other controlled sources
www.fsc.org Cert no. TT-COC-002641
© 1996 Forest Stewardship Council

FSC

ISBN: [paperback] 978-1-909671-24-9

eISBN: [mobi] 978-1-909671-25-6

Book design: Kathy Norman

Cover design: Paul Carney

ACKNOWLEDGMENTS

For all of us who think in pictures...

For all of us who doubt our idea is any good, undermine our own ability and question our worth...

I'd like to thank Paul Carney for all his hard work, effort and determination to write this book. You were wracked with self-doubt, were constantly out of your comfort zone and it felt like every word had to be checked and verified at times. You had very little support for this book, yet you perservered and got it finished.

The desire to prove that drawing is more than just a superficial, decorative skill for the gifted few, kept you going and forced you to really consider and empathise with students and teachers of other subject disciplines. I'd like to think that this book will elevate drawing's status as significant classroom tool for learning, because it should be right up there with writing.

Paul Carney

www.paulcarneyarts.com

January 2021

Dedication

This book is for all the students who find learning hard

CONTENTS

INTRODUCTION

If you can think it, you can draw it. If you can write it, you can draw it. Drawing is the manifestation of our internal thoughts. Where writing is a translation of thoughts into complex symbolic code, drawing is our thoughts visualised into pictorial imagery, a natural extension of what our brains are trying to achieve when we think.

Research by Fernandes, Wammes and Meade in 2018 assessed drawing as a learning strategy. They found that drawing information improved memory and was a very reliable way of boosting performance. Drawing enhances the learning of individual words and pictures as well as text. The learning gains they identified were greater from drawing than other known learning techniques such as reading and repeating things, writing or even copying information. Their conclusion was that drawing improves memory, and it does this because the physical act of drawing gets you to represent and describe the thoughts, images and visualisations in your mind.

The barrier to using drawing as a learning tool is that it is seen as an elitist skill for those lucky enough to have been born with natural talent. What I want to prove to you is that if you can write your name you can draw anything in this book. If you can draw a stick person you are good enough to use drawing for learning. I will not employ high level drawing skills beyond drawing the crudest, most basic of shapes or copying and tracing.

This book is going to show you how simply drawing stuff can help you learn things better. It will empower you to remember, process and understand things much more successfully. This is because drawing is a lot lot older than writing and in fact when we draw we are involving a lot more areas of our brain than if we simply write stuff down or say it. Our species have been drawing for at least a hundred thousand years, but writing is only a few thousand years old. In fact, writing originally developed from simple, symbolic drawings.

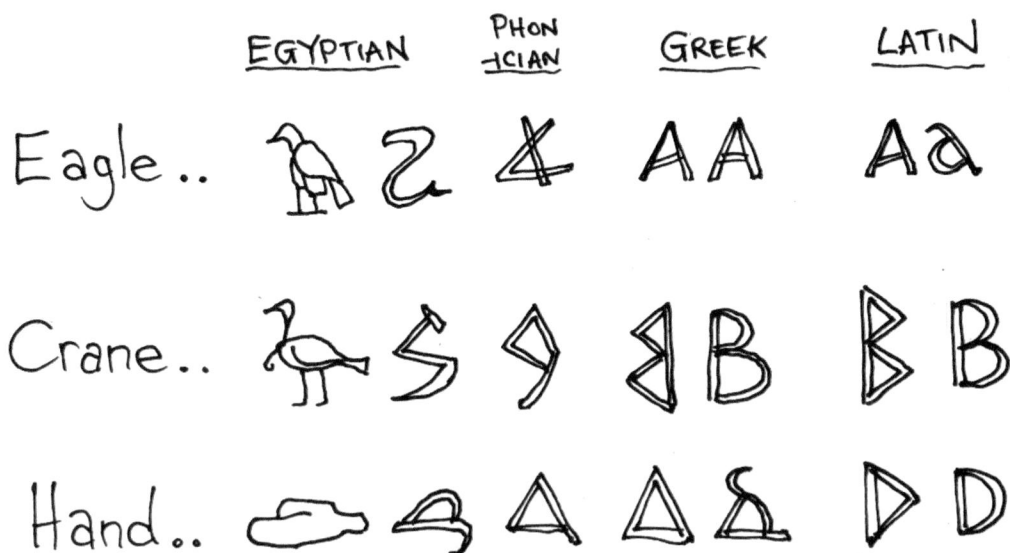

	EGYPTIAN	PHON-ICIAN	GREEK	LATIN
Eagle..				
Crane..				
Hand..				

Development of writing from Hieroglyphics to Latin symbols.

Incredibly, our children still learn to draw before they can write and still develop their writing skills from their drawing skills.

This book is not an art book, nor is it a book only for artists who can already draw. It's a book designed to help you in all subjects in the school: maths, English, history, geography, languages, science and others. It is a book for people who don't think they can draw. I have taught art for decades; I know that the very mention of drawing sets many people in a panic. They feel stupid when they draw and so they don't do it because they feel embarrassed. Don't be.

This wouldn't be much of a book about learning in all subjects if it required you to draw 'brilliantly' would it? So let's measure your drawing ability to see if you can use this book successfully.

1. EVERYONE CAN DRAW
You just might not know it yet

A drawing test

Please read the instructions carefully before you begin

Time allowed: all the time in the world.

Materials required: something to draw with and something to draw on.

Examination conditions: any time, any place, anywhere. Talking allowed, laughing encouraged.

The test

Write your name in the space provided.

The test is complete. Put your drawing implement down and stare out of the window for one hour and twenty-nine minutes.

Assessing the test

- **Can you read it?**

  Congratulations, you've passed the test. You can draw.

- **Mine can't be read.**

  Congratulations, you're an abstract artist.

- **I didn't write anything.**

  Congratulations, you're a conceptual artist.

- **I threw mine away and refused to do it.**

  You're a Turner Prize candidate.

Your drawing ability

As long as you can write your name you can use drawing to help you learn. This book is NOT about drawing like this:

Winter Crow,
*graphite on paper
by Paul Carney.*

It's about drawing like this:

One-minute bird drawings by adults and children.

As long as you can tell what it is then it is successful. But since this book depends on you doing some simple drawing, let me give you a few basic tips.

All writing is made up of quite simple shapes.

EFH   COQ PRT   A,MN   S
        GUBDJY   VWZ   f,s
             K
Letters are just   L   V,Z
             X
elaborations on   Y
simple geometric   a,b,c,d,e,g,h,
shapes.   q,r,u,t,x,w,
                    y,J,m,n,o,p,l,
                    t,v,z

As children, we learn how to draw shapes, then we learn how to turn the shapes into letters.

We learn to write by drawing familiar shapes.

Since all writing is made up of simple shapes such as circles, lines and triangles and we can all write, then it's safe to assume we can all draw simple shapes. So would it surprise you to learn that everything you see in the world around you is made up of those same simple shapes?

Identifying letter shapes around you

Go for a walk around your house. Look at all the things you find and try to identify the letter shapes that make them up. Don't try to draw the things you see, just look at them and think about the letter shapes you can see. If you don't see any letter shapes, then just look for basic shapes such as squares and rectangles.

- Now go out in your street and do the same thing.

- Now go where there are lots of natural things like bushes, trees, grass etc. and do the same again.

- Now look at yourself, your friends or family and do it again.

- Finally, look at pictures of animals and find the shapes they are made of.

Everything you see is composed from the same simple shapes we use everyday to write with. So if we can write our name we can draw anything.

Still not convinced? Okay, let's investigate this further.

Drawing with letters

You can draw these two example pictures with letter shapes.

Objects can be constructed from simple letter shapes.

The cup can be drawn with the letters O, I and D.

These headphones can be drawn with the letter O, ovals and circles.

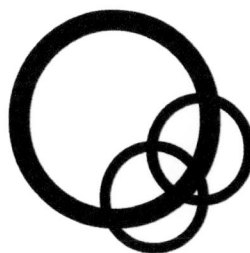

Practice drawing more things with letters. Begin with simple objects then get progressively more complex.

Simple drawing

Nearly everyone draws cartoons as a kid. Then art teachers come along and tell you they aren't proper art. But I'm an art teacher and they are, so there! This style of drawing is called 'glyphic' drawing and it involves drawing things with simple outlines using simple shapes. We can build on our first lessons of drawing using letters to begin drawing using the simple shapes that letters are made up from: circles, triangles, squares and wavy lines.

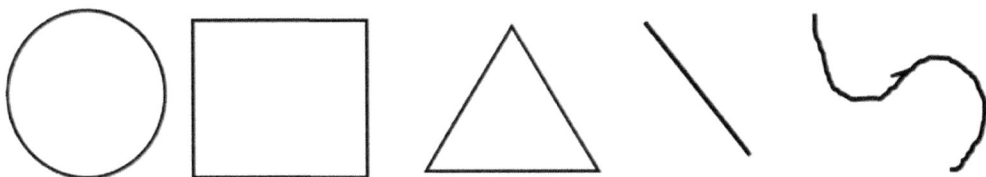

Believe it or not, but these simple shapes make up everything in the world around us. It might be difficult at first, but eventually you'll learn what the French artist Paul Cezanne said in 1896: *'Everything in nature can be reduced to the simple sphere, cone or cylinder'.*

Most 'how to draw' books show you that you can draw animals and people and cars and all kinds of things with just a few simple circles, squares and lines.

Remember, in this book all you're trying to do is to draw to communicate the meaning of what it is – not to draw artistically. You can even just draw stick people if you like, so this level of drawing is perfect!

A stick person is made up of a circle and a few straight lines; what we refer to in writing as I's and O's.

If you can draw a stick person you can draw anything.

But a few circles more can create a pig!

Or a dog. Or a cow. You get the idea…

In this way, a rectangle can become a door or you can join circles and rectangles up to make cars, lorries, keys or people.

Most people can draw like this but they don't think this is 'proper' drawing, and they are so embarrassed by it they don't do it. But this IS drawing! All you will need to do these exercises is to be able to draw to the standard we have just covered.

Lesson: I'd like you to copy these drawings then try to draw a few more animals or objects of your own.

Copy these simple pictures then make up some of your own.

You may need to draw very specific things such as emotions on people's faces, hands or people which can seem pretty daunting at first. To draw people, draw stick people whenever you feel you can't draw a cartoon person.

To draw hands, just draw three fingers and don't worry about them looking realistic.

So long as you can recognise your own drawings they are 'good enough'.

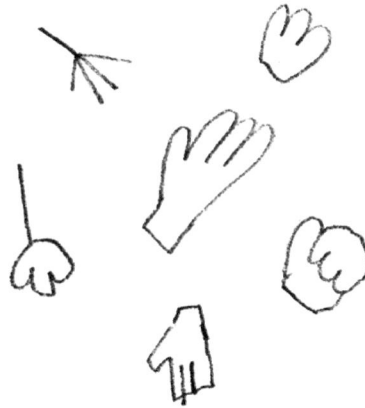

To draw faces, just draw simple emojis like these:

Drawing lines

This might seem a little odd, but I'd like you to practice drawing straight lines without a ruler. Try to draw them quickly but draw them accurately. Do them again and again and again and again, because when you can draw lines easily and accurately, you will be able to draw much better.

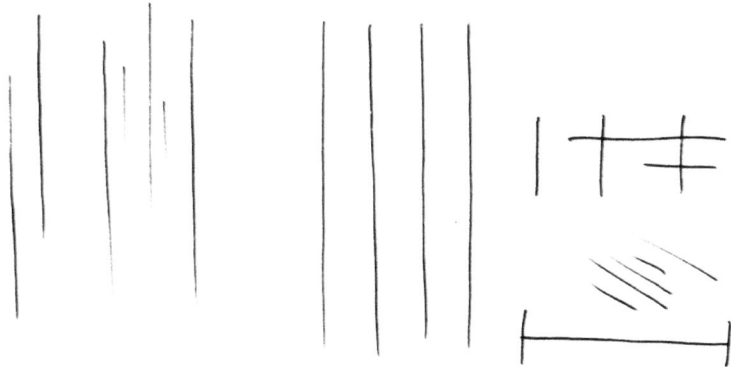

Drawing lines is a great practice exercise.

Keep doing this and try making patterns and doodles using straight lines. When you feel confident, I'd like you to try drawing a square grid, keeping all of your lines straight and equidistant.

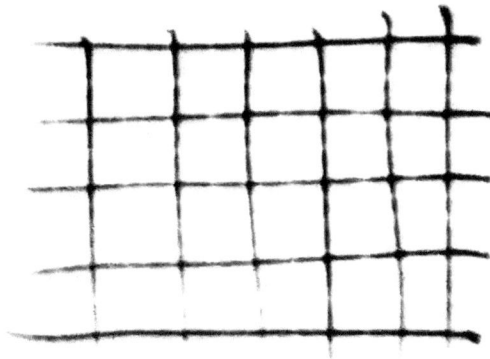

Next, I'd like you to draw more lines and then divide them into equal portions just by using your eye and judgment, no rulers please!

Divide lines into two equal pieces, then four, five, six etc. Keep going and going until you improve and get better at doing it. What you're learning to do is the artist's technique of measuring visually. When they draw, artists are naturally measuring the length and size of shapes in relation to each other, they are gauging and estimating spaces, trying to replicate the mathematical proportions of the objects they see before them. When you can do this well, and do it easily, without thinking, you will become a much more skilled artist.

Estimating proportions and measurements is a key component of drawing complex forms.

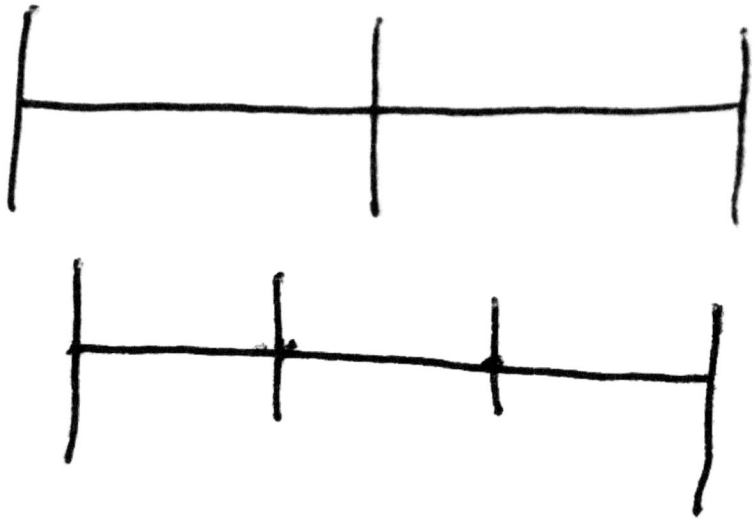

Playing with letter patterns

Simply making patterns from letter forms helps you, not only to draw better, but to improve your maths skills too! This is because to create patterns you are rotating, transforming, flipping, inverting, reflecting and adapting the letter forms, which is exactly what you are taught to do in maths lessons! This kind of adaptability with shapes is really important to drawing and drawing patterns is so cool.

Write your name in capital letters on a piece of paper. Draw mirror image versions of the letters and join them together to make new shapes. You can flip the shapes, turn them upside down, stretch or bend them. It's up to you.

Playing with patterns is a super way to develop your drawing skills and it's fun.

PAUL CARNEY

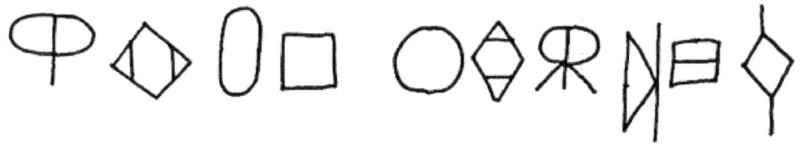

Next, select some interesting letter shapes and make them into a repeat pattern.

You can make some interesting patterns from letter shapes.

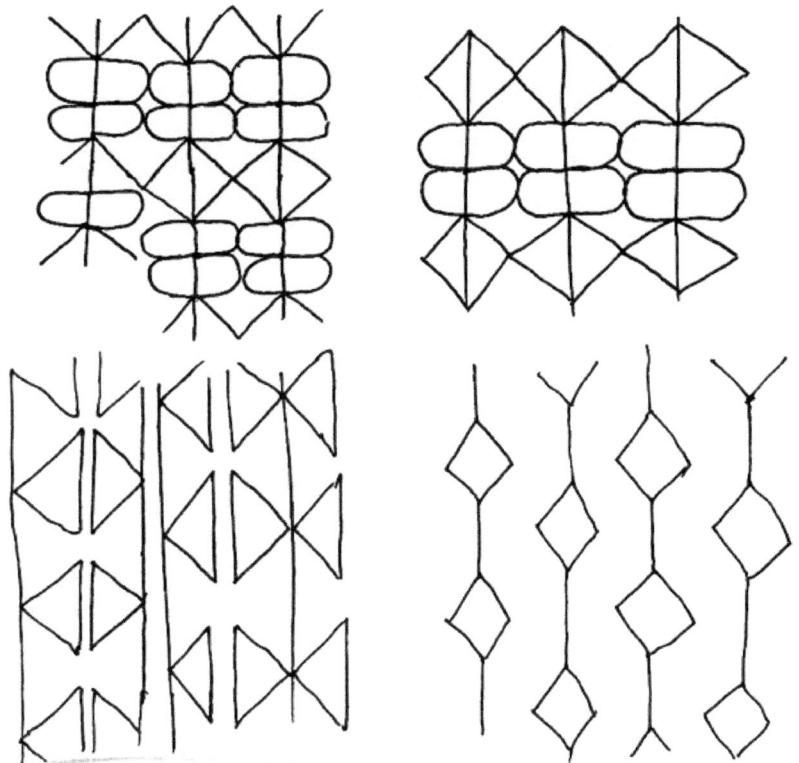

Play with more letter shapes to make patterns. I can do this forever and not get bored, but maybe I need a social life!

23

Handwriting drawing - controlled scribbles

Handwriting, where we join letters into single flowing lines, is an advanced stage of writing. It's also advanced drawing. When you learn handwriting, you are learning to write fluently with long, single lines. We use exactly this same skill when we draw too, so let's explore this connection.

Practice writing your name. Then write it continuously, repeating it on a single line without stopping. Then stop writing it on a straight line and allow it to 'deconstruct' like a gas vaporising on the page.

Take your handwriting for a walk.

Break letters down into scribbles.

Press hard, then press light. Play with the line.

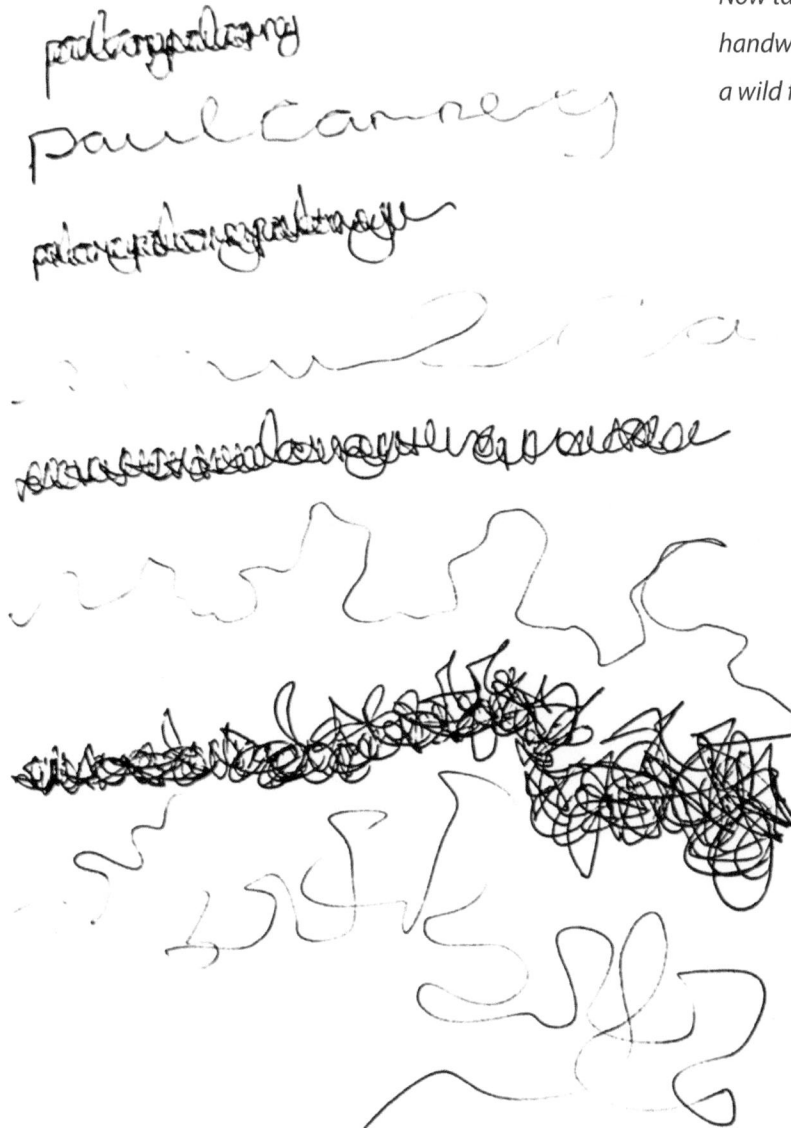

*Now take your
handwriting on
a wild frenzy!*

Then select a photo you like and try to draw it using your continuous handwriting style and the letters of your name. Keep doing this often. Think of it like controlling a scribble, because that's all it is.

Layout

It is difficult to understand something if it is set out badly like this:

Our brains struggle to make sense of information that is poorly laid out.

That is why we set writing out in straight lines either horizontally or vertically and read from either left to right or right to left, and top to bottom or bottom to top, depending on your culture.

COMMUNICATION   NOITACINUMMOC

C
O
M
M
U
N
I
C
A
T
I
O
N

COMMUNICATION

When setting out drawings on a page, think about how it will be 'read'. Try to imagine you are setting out multiple drawings for a comic, where chunks of information are laid out in separate boxes. You can draw lines around the boxes or leave spaces, it's up to you, but once you get the hang of it you won't need the boxes as much.

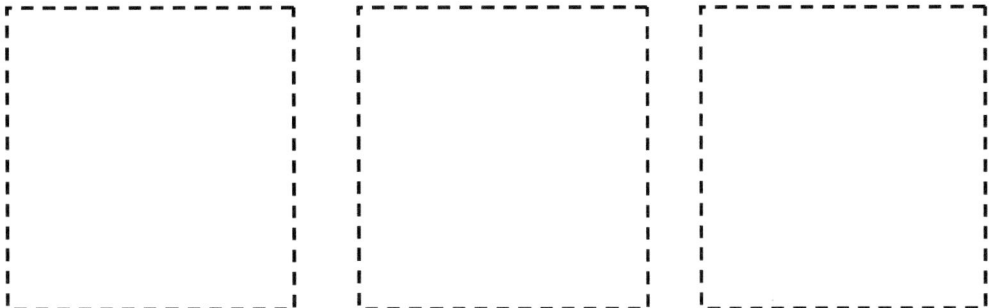

27

The first drawing is set out well and is easy to follow. The second is muddled and confusing.

Tips & Techniques

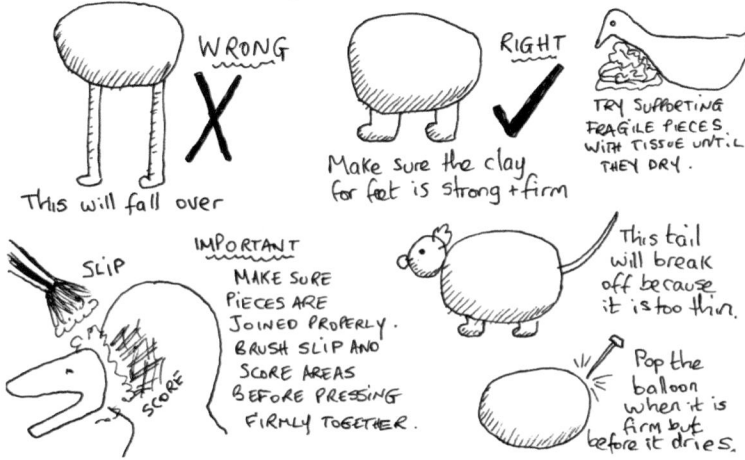

WRONG X
This will fall over

RIGHT ✓
Make sure the clay for feet is strong + firm

TRY SUPPORTING FRAGILE PIECES WITH TISSUE UNTIL THEY DRY.

SLIP

IMPORTANT
MAKE SURE PIECES ARE JOINED PROPERLY. BRUSH SLIP AND SCORE AREAS BEFORE PRESSING FIRMLY TOGETHER.

SCORE

This tail will break off because it is too thin.

Pop the balloon when it is firm but before it dries.

If you need to set lots of things out clearly then sometimes it helps to use an imaginary grid on your paper. Artists often use a 3-column grid like this:

Grids like this are a traditional way to set out information so it is legible.

Or a 4-column grid like this:

But you can use any size grid you like to set things out. You don't have to keep exactly to these grid lines, they are just there to help you.

Summary

You don't need amazing drawing skills to be able to use drawing to learn.

If you can write your name you can draw anything, because everything is made up of simple shapes and letter shapes.

When you learned handwriting, you learned how to join separate shapes up into long, flowing lines. Drawing is a more open, less controlled version of handwriting.

If we want to be able to understand our drawings later, we need to set them out neatly and in order so they don't get muddled up and confusing.

How I do my drawings

I begin by making a quick sketch in my sketchbook. Sometimes I'll do two or three to get it right.

Try to draw naturally, without concern for correctness, then render your drawings with black pen.

Then I'll draw it out neatly on a new sheet of paper and adapt and improve it as I go.

Then I'll go over the lines with a fineliner again, changing and improving it as I go. This means I've drawn the image at least three times, which helps me remember it even more effectively.

Then I need to rub out my pencil lines and clean it up.

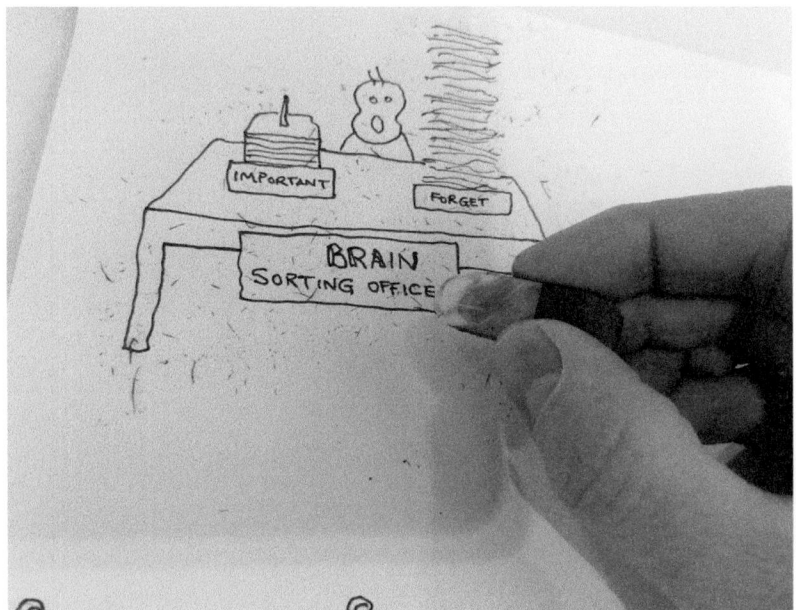

2. MEMORY EXPLAINED

Information is everywhere, all around us, all the time. It bombards our senses and even when we sleep, we are processing it. Information comes to us via our senses of sight, hearing, smell, touch and taste. It is then processed by our brains, but much of this is done automatically without us even having to think about it.

My brain being bombarded with information.

Memories are stored in only the top thin outer layer of our brain in huge, microscopic networks of neurons. These transmit information as electrical energy and they can grow stronger connections between each other the more we use them.

FOUR memory types

To remember things we have a quick, flash memory called **sensory memory**. This lasts a few milliseconds, but it gives us a quick impression of a new event.

Then we have **short-term memory** which is usually the last 20 seconds of what you experience. We can usually hold around 4 to 6 items in short-term memory, any more than that and you begin forgetting things.

Long-term memory is made up of events and information we hold in our brain over longer periods. We constantly refer to this kind of memory to help us make decisions, so it is important.

Working memory is a kind of constant, flowing operation combining all forms of memory. It is how we make decisions, solve problems and understand what is going on in the world. Our working memory draws on information we have stored up, including any emotions we have about it, to help us.

Drawing: *Make a quick drawing of a person playing a computer game. Any game will suffice, but I've chosen FIFA soccer. Can you visualise how the different types of memory might be used to play the game?*

What quick, sensory information might you get about the game upon first glance? *(Colours of the strips and pitch, sounds, emotions.)*

What things would you have in your short-term memory to play the game? *(Rules of the game, how to move your fingers on the controller, names of players, where the players are, where the ball is.)*

What information would be in your long-term memory? *(Past games you've played, how certain players behave, tactics they use against you, previous score lines, sound effects, graphics.)*

How would you use working memory to play the game? *(To move the controller to put the players where you want them to be, to make the players behave as you want them. You would do this based on your previous experiences of how to play the game.)*

What other factors might affect your memory as you play the game? *(You might get stuck on something you have been stuck on before, things can put you off, distractions etc.)*

Memory for learning

School-based learning depends largely on taking information in through the senses and making secure memories from it that can be recalled at a future date. It's not much good if you think you know it then forget it later!

Your brain doesn't want to carry lots of information in short-term memory, so it only holds what it needs and stores the rest in long-term memory or forgets it.

Our brains don't want to carry lots of irrelevant material in working memory because it's too hard.

The other annoying thing about information in the brain is the way it is stored. Information in the brain is quite chaotic, more like a teenager's bedroom or a messy garage than a neat filing system.

We don't remember things in neat, organised bundles, but rather in random, chaotic ways.

There's lots of half-remembered, vague bits of memories (like finding half-eaten sweets under your bed) and things are stored in bizarre and weird ways such as things that are red, shiny things, hard metal things, horrible things and things that smell like poo. And it gets even more chaotic than that, because new information is coming in all the time and most of it isn't even labelled or tagged. Things get put in the wrong place and if they aren't used much then the brain piles lots of new stuff on top of them, until you can't find them for love nor money.

This isn't the brain's fault; it has been brilliant for millions of years thank you very much. It assigns nice feelings and emotions to things that you like and are good for you and bad ones to things that might hurt or upset you. It can spot danger by sight, hearing, touch, taste or smell and knows what will cut, burn or sting you. It remembers important stuff like how hot fire is or how cold snow is and makes sure it remembers nasty people who do nasty things because it wants to avoid them in the future.

Remembering that Poland has a unitary semi-presidential constitutional republic isn't high on its list of priorities. This type of knowledge is something we human beings have invented, and we have to work hard if we want to learn it effectively because as I said earlier, your brain muddles things up and forgets things.

Our brain sorting office has a huge pile labelled 'forget'.

Memory pizzas

So why are some people really good at remembering stuff and others aren't? Why do you forget things as soon as you've been told them when the class swot only needs to hear it once and it's in their brain forever?

Well this is probably best explained through pizza.

Memory works a lot like a pizza delivery service, only delivering information instead of pizzas. It works okay when there is the right amount of pizza, delivery drivers and customers.

Knowledge is made up things humans have learned, discovered or invented.

But if you don't have enough drivers or pizzas then customers will get frustrated.

Sometimes the demand to remember knowledge is greater
than our capacity to store and deliver it on time.

This sounds straightforward: so long as you keep making the pizzas and delivering them you will be fine. But think about what it's like at school. You don't just do maths all day do you? No, you do a bit of maths, then some English, then science, a bit of art, history, geography and if that wasn't enough, all sorts of other information is pouring in such as who is on first dinner sitting? what happened with Liam Jenkins in Mrs Dodd's class? what's on TV tonight? etc. etc. etc. etc.

In our pizza analogy the pizza shop can't just sell pizzas, it must sell Chinese food, Indian, Lebanese, fish and chips, burgers, kebabs and lots of other things too. And it must deliver them on time, to the right people at the right temperature because customers get annoyed if their order is wrong and teachers get upset if you fail an exam!

Our pizza analogy has to be expanded to include different knowledge foodstuffs going to different locations.

The solution to this chaos then is to improve the delivery service and organise the take-away food properly in the first place. You can improve your own pizza delivery service (memory) by using things that help you to remember. This might be drawing or might be lots of other stuff too, such as repeating information or using acrostics or whatever helps. And just by remembering it effectively in the first place it will be easier to find and retrieve when you want it.

Some people have bigger neural 'roads' that carry information really quickly for certain types of information.

What makes all of this even more unfair is that some people are born with efficient pizza super-highways (this is called white matter in your brain) connecting their knowledge pizzas (grey matter) to customers, and people with more white matter super-highways can learn things more quickly and can retrieve information more efficiently. Other people have less white matter like single track country roads and so have to work much harder to store and retrieve information from their grey matter. This might sound incredibly unfair (it is!) but remember I said that this type of information is only one type of many.

Other people seem to have country lanes that move information more slowly, but remember we have different sized 'roads' for different things.

Some people might have single track roads for English lessons but super-highways for maths and vice versa. Some might have super-highways for playing football or art, for example. Who decides which is most important?

If that was the end of the story we could just identify which things we have the best pizza highways for and then specialise in that area, but life, as ever, is much more complicated. This is because the brain can grow new connections. Just as we can build new roads to make them more efficient, so we can build better information stores in our brains and construct more efficient routes between them.

We can grow new pathways in our brains to learn new things, but it takes time, patience and persistence.

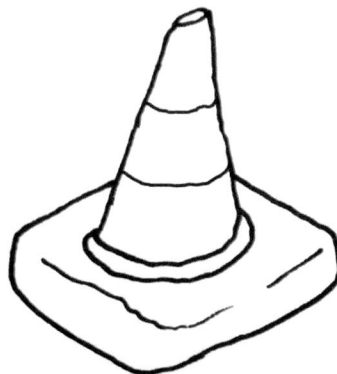

This isn't easy and it takes resources, time and patience, especially when some brain box learns things faster than you can say them, but you can do it if you do it slowly, regularly and you're motivated.

Building new stores of grey matter and making the white matter connections between them is called learning. You are learning all the time you are alive, whether you want to or not, but school selects information it thinks is most important to you and concentrates on teaching you that.

Schools know that some people are naturally better at learning some types of stuff than others and they are constantly looking for ways to help those that struggle so that everyone can learn. But one method that is really showing itself to be effective is drawing, and as a drawing expert I want to show you how it can help you.

I hope you've practiced the drawing exercises in chapter one, I also hope you have an open mind to try something new and that you are not going to give up too soon. You may have some negative experiences of drawing, people might have belittled you about your drawing (sometimes teachers do that and it makes me so angry), but we are going to overcome that and give it our best, aren't we?

Memories are often fragmented and incomplete. We need to devote time and practice to improve our recall.

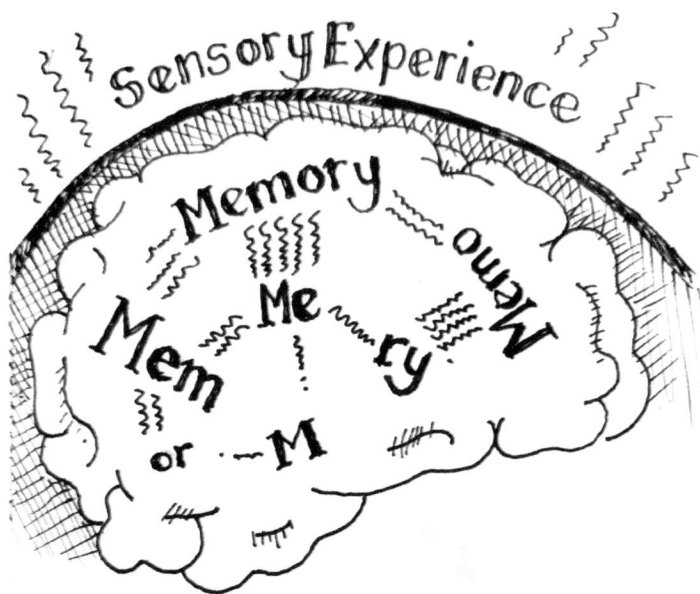

My answers to the drawing question

This is me playing a computer game. Sensory memory gives me a quick impression of the game, short-term memory helps me remember what's happening in the game now, working memory helps me make decisions about what to do next and long-term memory helps me remember what things happened in previous games.

This is me playing the FIFA soccer computer game really badly.

3. BASIC TECHNIQUES OF MEMORY DRAWING

Technique 1: Syllable Sound Association Drawing (SSAD)

You will no doubt be familiar with some memory strategies you use to help you remember things. I LOVE acronyms and acrostics (where you make a word up from the first letters of words), I like to repeat things and say them out loud, but most of all I love to draw to remember.

This technique is great whenever you need to learn lots of language, such as scientific or mathematical words, or terminology in Geography or Design and Technology. When all these add up there can be so many words to remember it can become very confusing.

One way of remembering is to break the complex word down into syllables then associate drawn images to each syllable sound. Making associations and connections between things you already know and things you want to learn is really powerful. The more vivid and unusual you can make these links the better and this is where drawing comes in.

Take for example some common words from science texts. It can be difficult to remember all of these complex words, yet you really need to know them before you can really understand what they do.

Let's list a few common ones: protein, amino, vitamins, minerals, carbohydrate and let's begin one at a time and break these complicated words down into syllable sounds and pictures.

Protein can be broken down into pro-tein. Can you think of pictures to associate with these smaller sounds?

I can think of these, but you might have your own.

Protein

Pro = a professional footballer or sportsperson.

Tein = a teenager.

Amino

Am = I'm thinking of a.m. in the morning which could be a sunrise or a clock with a.m. on it.

Min = sounds like mean, so I could draw a mean looking face.

No = a big cross or a hand outstretched.

Vitamins

Vit = I can't think of anything for Vit, so I will use a big letter V and the word hit, represented by a face being hit.

Am = I'll use my same drawing from the Am in the word amino.

In = I could draw a sign saying In or even an old pub sign that says 'Inne'.

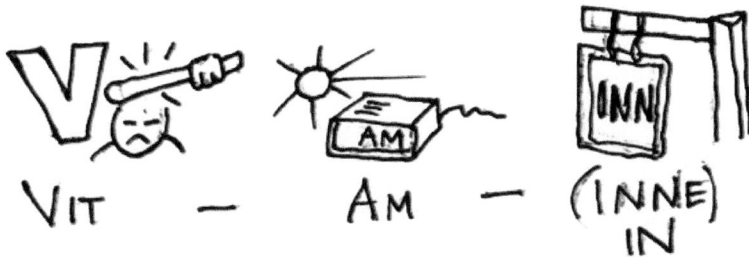

Minerals

Min = I'm going to change this slightly to be a 'mean' face drawing because I can remember that easily and it sounds like Min.

Er = I could draw hair.

Al = a hall.

Carbohydrate

Car = a car.

Bo = Bo Peep.

Hyd = someone hiding.

Rate = a film rating or heart rate or even just a ray of sunshine.

CAR - BO - (HIDE) - RATE
HYD

This method can be tricky at first, because sometimes it's hard to think of pictures for each sound. It gets easier the more you do it because the same sounds pop up time and time again and you can repeat them.

Also, you should try to highlight the first letter of each word because you will think of that first, before anything else. In the word Amino I could have used a picture of Ham for the first part, but I know from experience that this would confuse me when I tried to remember it because I'd think of the H first and not the A.

BUT WAIT A MINUTE!

This method is very good at helping you to remember difficult words in any lesson, but you need to remember the meaning of the word too!

To do this you need to do another drawing to associate the meaning of the word. For example PROTEIN now becomes:

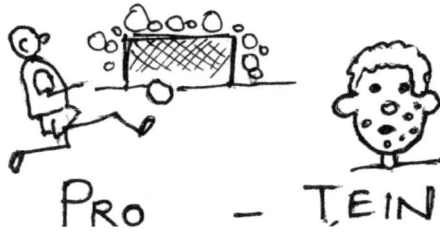

PRO — TEIN

=

BUILDING BLOCKS

AM — (MEAN) — NO
MIN

=

9 AMINO ACIDS
MAKE PROTEIN

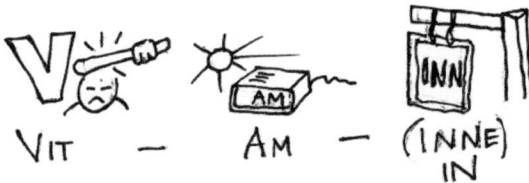

VIT — AM — (INNE)
IN

=

KEEP YOU

HEALTHY

(MEAN) — (HAIR) — (HALL)
MIN — ER — AL

=

BALANCED DIET

CAR — BO — (HIDE) — RATE
HYD

=

ENERGY

You may have noticed that there are two ways of representing a syllable sound. We can either draw what it means or draw how it sounds. For example, the word 'heat' could use a drawing to represent hot, or to eat food:

You could use either of these drawings to represent 'heat' but I prefer to keep the meaning of the word.

Heat   Eat

Of course, either way is fine, and I use both, but I would prefer to use the hot sun drawing because it preserves the meaning of the word.

Okay now it's your turn. I'm going to give you some words and I want you to try to draw an image associated with the sound of the syllables. Let's start with some easy ones:

Light	**Lap**	**Pain**
Nut	**Dot**	**Sack**

Now let's make it harder:

Planter	**Cupboard**	**Gaseous**
Bottle	**Wooden**	**Tumble**

And harder:

Enchanted	**Lizard**	**Ornament**
Turntable	**Capillary**	**Sedimentary**

And even harder:

Psychology **Uterosacral ligament** **Blastocyst**

Vascular **Igneous** **Fimbriae**

Vowel sounds

You will encounter the same syllable sounds again and again using this method and no more so than with vowel sounds. The letter A for example, has a hard 'hay' sound, but also a softer 'ah' sound as in spa. The letter E can be a long 'eee' as in emu or an 'eh' sound as in egg. The letter I can be spoken as 'eye' or a harder 'I' as in sin. O can be 'oh' as in roll, or 'o' as in long, but also 'ooh' as in tool. The U in unicorn is spoken differently to the u in under.

So it is a good idea to have some basic sounds sorted out before you begin using the SSAD method. Here are some examples I did, copy them, then add more to make a full list of vowel sounds.

Make drawings of common sounds you use over and over again such as vowels.

A = 🌾 HAY [OR] 👄 Aah

E = 😫 He He He [OR] 🥚 Egg

I = 👁 EYE [OR] 🪟 INNE INNE

O = 🧹 HOE [OR] 🔥 HOT

U = 🐑 EWE [OR] ⬆ UP

Getting stuck

At times, you can't think of any picture at all because the syllable sound is so strange. Numbers are like this because they have their roots in Arabic, Hindu and Persian languages. Look the word up in the dictionary, look in a thesaurus or a rhyming dictionary and give yourself time to work it out. If you can't think of anything, just draw the first letter, then add something that sounds like the syllable sound. For example:

If you're really stuck just think of a word that rhymes with the syllable sound then add a big letter at the beginning. When trying to recall words, you'll likely remember the first letter of the word before anything else.

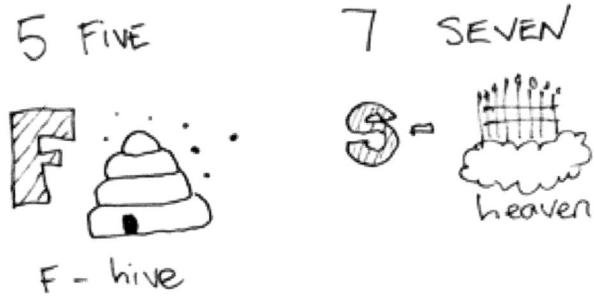

5 FIVE

F - hive

7 SEVEN

S - heaven

Or you might draw complex words like this:

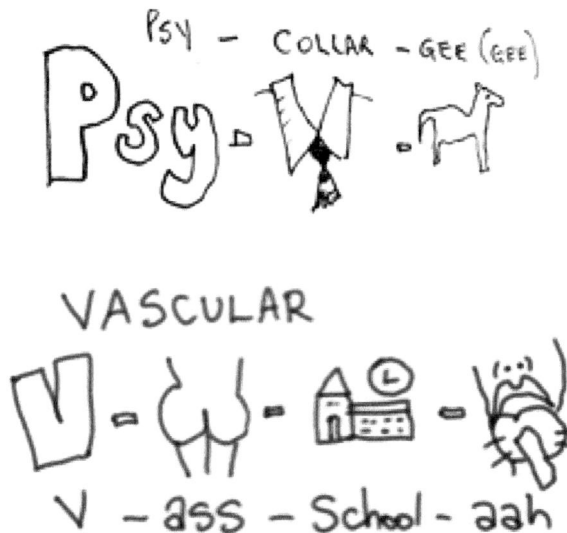

PSY - COLLAR - GEE (GEE)

Psy - V - 𝗑

VASCULAR

V - ass - School - aah

Numbers

You can use the SSAD technique to remember numbers, however they have strange Arabic derivatives and are harder to find associations for. You might want to adopt mine if you can't think of your own, so copy these out.

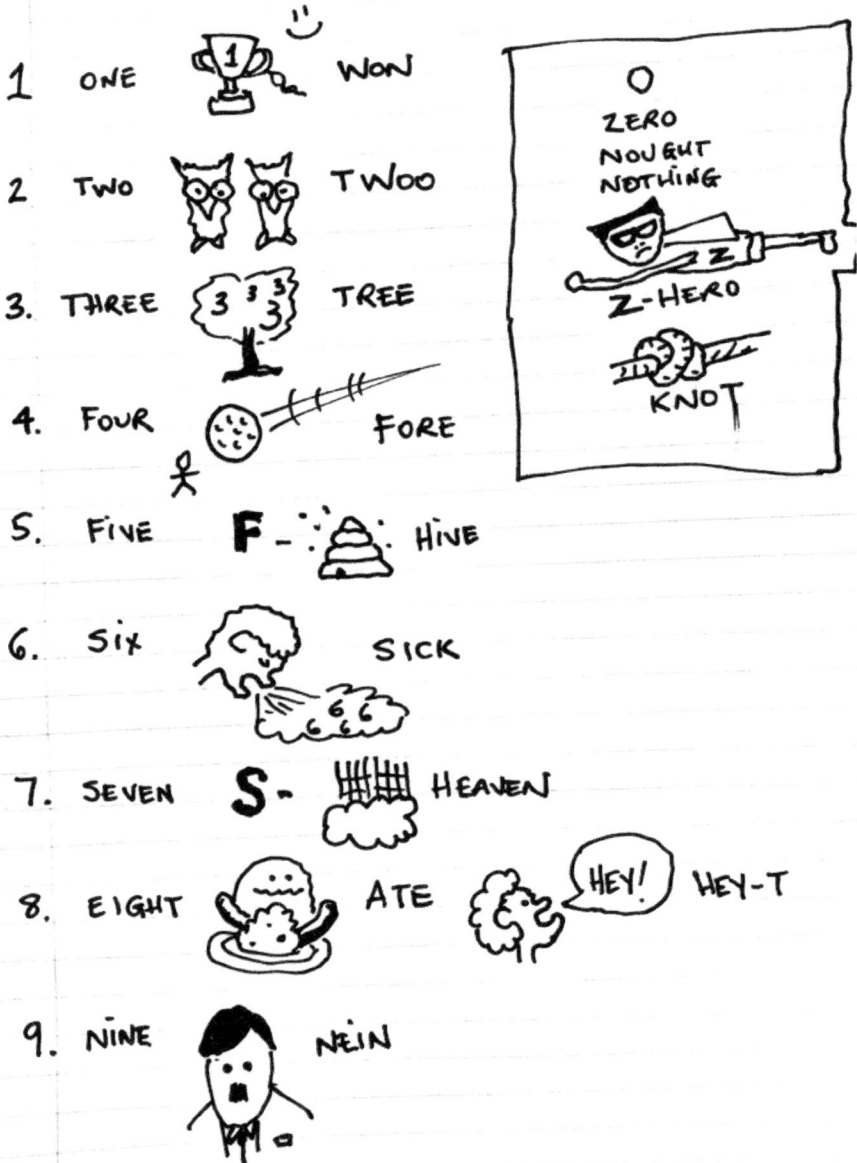

I've drawn these number associations on lined paper and that's fine!
Use them anywhere and everywhere to help you remember things.

Then of course you'll need to learn the tens. I would just use the ten number along with the following digit such as three or four to make thirteen or fourteen for example. If this doesn't work for you, then feel free to make up your own.

10 TEN	TEN PIN HEN	
20 TWENTY	TWIN	TEA
30 THIRTY	THIRSTY	
40 FORTY	FORT	TEA
50 FIFTY	FIFE	TEA
60 SIXTY	SICK	
70 SEVENTY	S - HEAVEN	TEA
80 EIGHTY	HATE ATE	TEA
90 NINETY	NEIN	TEA
HUNDRED	HUN	DREDD DREDS

Some numbers are really hard to find syllable associations for, such as twenty, thirty, fifty, so try to draw pictures that sound like the word, such as twins for twenty.

Once you have learned the syllable sound association drawings for numbers you can use it to learn all kinds of stuff. I find that I'm always forgetting some of my times tables, such as nine times seven or nine times eight, so I can now draw the ones I'm stuck on using SSAD techniques. I wouldn't do this for all the times tables, just the ones I'm struggling with.

By writing the numbers as symbols as well as drawing them you are employing dual coding techniques which should help you remember them even better.

$$9 \times 7 = 63$$

NEIN x HEAVEN = SICK TREE

$$9 \times 8 = 72$$

NEIN   ATE

SEVEN   TWOO

I would add an extra drawing to associate the number with a bank account or phone number so that the link is stronger.

3 7 5 6 2 4 1

3   7   5   6   2   4   1

The system might also be used to help you learn long numbers such as telephone numbers, bank codes, passwords or account numbers.

We can also use a variation on SSAD drawing to break down sentences, understanding and memorising them as we draw.

Qu'est-ce que tu veux manger ?
(KESS - KUH TEW VOO MON-JAY)

Deconstructing sentences using drawing is really
helpful for memory and understanding.

PORK-WAH ESS-KUH TEW PLUR

Technique 2: Decorative drawing

We might adapt our SSAD drawing in another way, by embedding our pictorial mnemonics into decorative, illustrated letters that spell out the word. This might be used to memorise individual words, or verbs in languages.

il = He

I've drawn each part of the verb using bubble letters (favoured by non-skilled artists,) then filled them with drawings depicting the meaning of the word. Notice how I have decorated the edges of the lettering. This helps me slowly absorb the shape of the word. I was speaking these out loud also as I was drawing them.

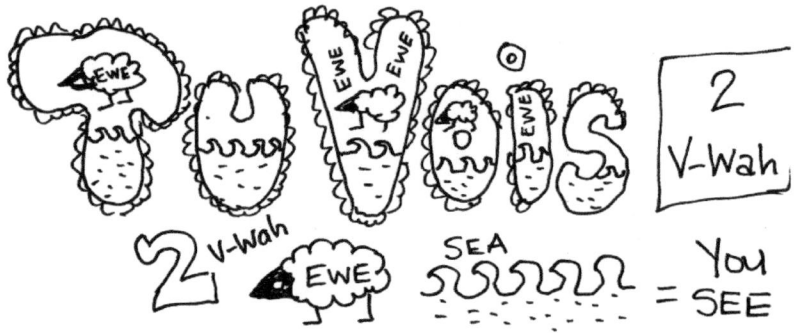

55

Technique 3: Meaning manipulation

I said that drawing improves memory, that the physical act of drawing gets you to represent and describe the thoughts, images and visualisations in your mind. So how do we draw to remember?

This is a simple exercise that you could use to help you to remember difficult words or learn subject terminology. All you have to do is to draw the meaning of the word using the letters of the word and a few, minimal additional drawings.

For example: DISSOLVE

I've tried to show the letters dissolving into a glass of water.

More science examples:

This exercise is a great way to learn key subject vocabulary.

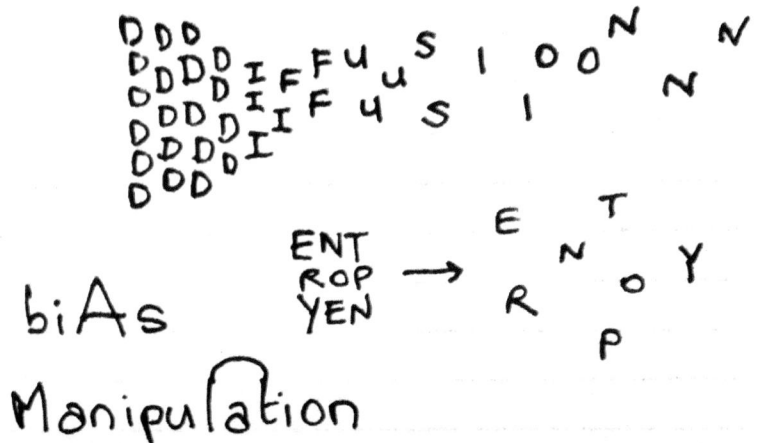

And some geography farming methods:

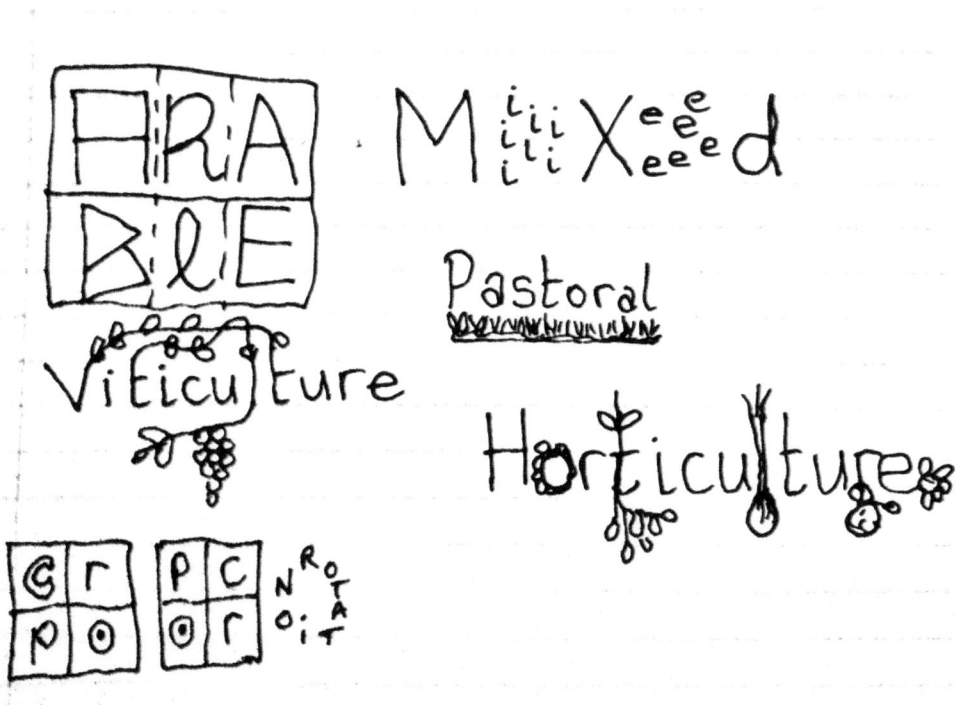

Spaced retrieval

You must remember that it doesn't matter how good or bad your drawings are, what matters is that you are drawing them!

You can use these methods to remember lots of complicated words and it works well, but like anything, they aren't magic. The way you will remember the words more effectively is if you repeat them and especially if you repeat them in intervals. The method that I find works well is to give myself intervals of ones: one minute, one hour, one day, one week, one month.

I draw the mnemonic first then close my book and think of something else for a minute. Then I'll try to draw it again without looking. I can now open my book and check my second answer. It's okay at this stage to copy the first example again if you need to, because you are just learning and need to get it right.

Now repeat this in about an hour or at the end of a lesson if it's more convenient. Repeat it again the next day, then in a week, then in a month. When you can recall and draw the list easily, without needing to look back at your first drawings, you can say you've remembered it.

However, don't be too confident just yet. Remember, your memory operates by forgetting stuff it doesn't need. You are much more likely to be able to recall this stuff if it is important to you and you use it a lot. We can easily become confident that we know things in the moment, but later, when we need it, it's gone. Exam stress and pressure does this to our brains, and I find that the song lyrics I have spent ages learning can disappear when I go onstage and am faced with an audience.

Go easy on yourself. It is very likely that you will forget stuff a lot, you're made that way after all, but keep revising, going over things and drawing those little pictures again and again to help you. The more you do them, the more you use them the easier it will be, but nothing is one hundred percent fool proof.

SSAD (Syllable Sound Association Drawing) summary

- Read the word and break it up into smaller syllables.

- Make visual connections in your mind with the sounds of these syllables.

- Draw the visual associations and write the word underneath.

- Make sure you draw a connection to the meaning of the word.

- Spend a short time trying to remember the words then cover them.

- After one minute: draw the words and pictures from memory.

- Repeat this after one hour, one day, one week, one month.

Drawing for memory examples

Here are some examples from my own notebook where I was studying genotypes and phenotypes in biology.

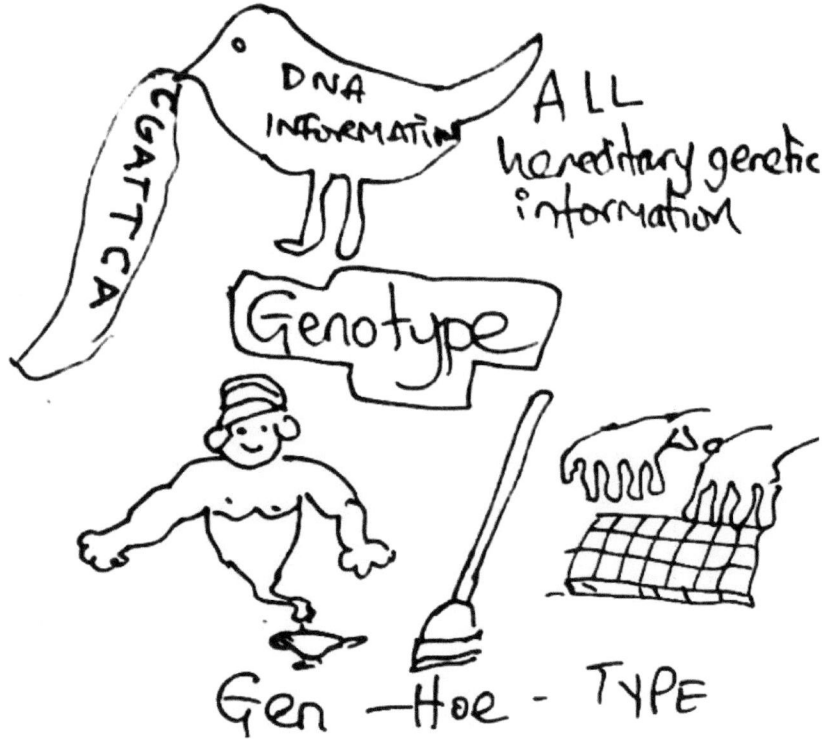

Drawing the difference between genotype and phenotype.

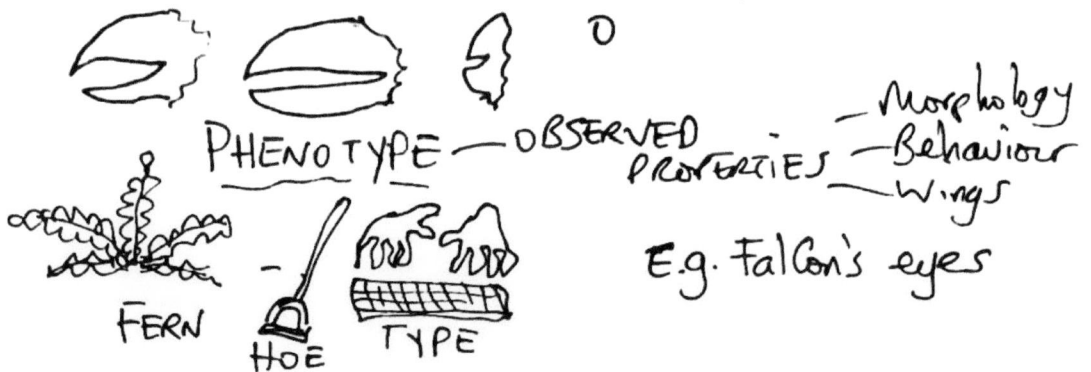

The SSAD (Syllable Sound Association Drawing) technique in a nutshell

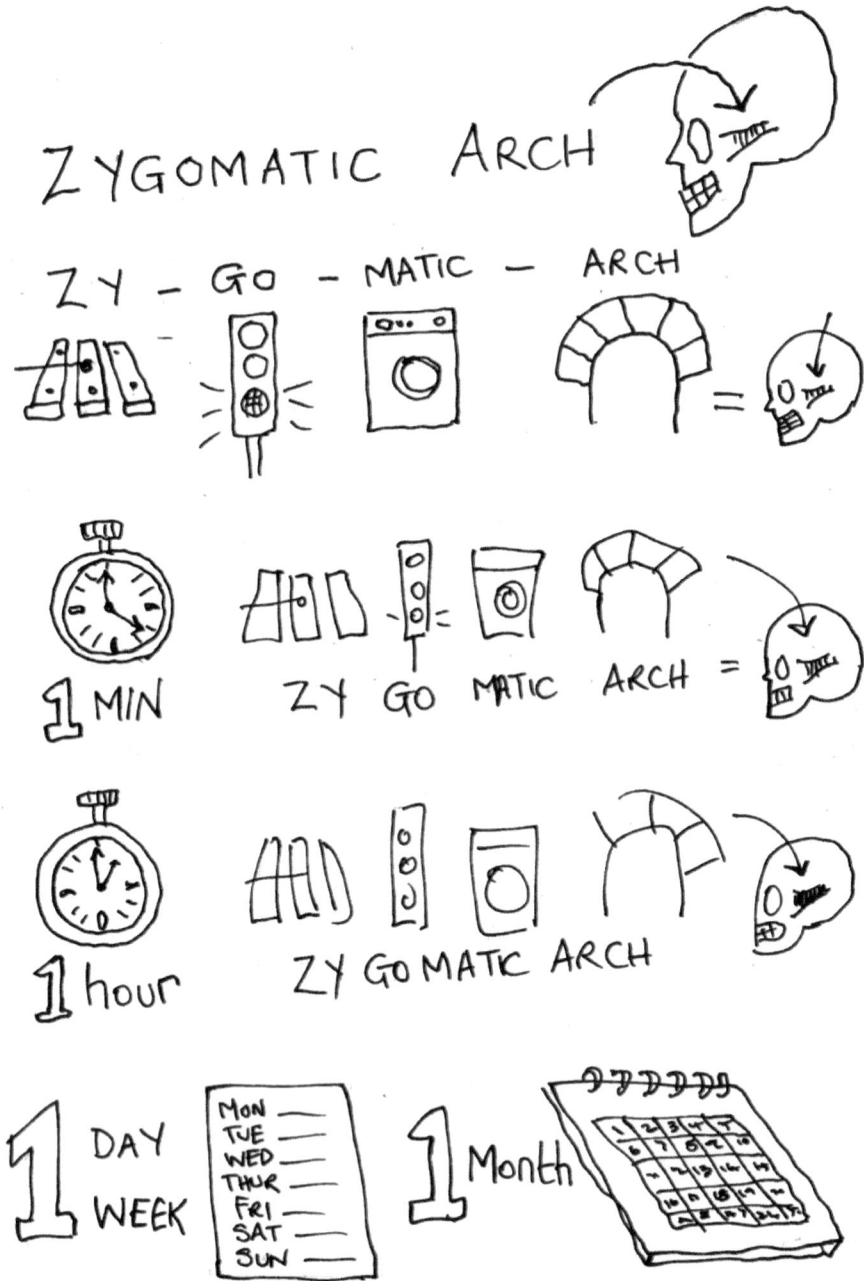

ZYGOMATIC ARCH

ZY – GO – MATIC – ARCH

1 MIN   ZY GO MATIC ARCH =

1 hour   ZY GO MATIC ARCH

1 DAY / WEEK

1 Month

It is important to redraw the mnemonic in spaced intervals.

Drawing for Learning in practice

The brilliant anatomist and artist Professor Alice Roberts has produced a series of wonderful videos on YouTube, teaching anatomy through drawing. It occurs to me that anatomy students could follow her videos and draw alongside her to learn her lesson through drawing. How amazing that would be, and it wouldn't matter what the quality of her students drawings was, they would all improve their learning simply through the act of drawing.

I decided to practice my SSAD drawing techniques using a part of her lecture. I have no prior nominal experience, so everything was new to me, and some of the language was very hard for me to process.

However, I drew along with her video Lockdown Embryology #9 Abdominal organs: https://youtu.be/kluDvUIEb5o

Her drawing turned out like this:

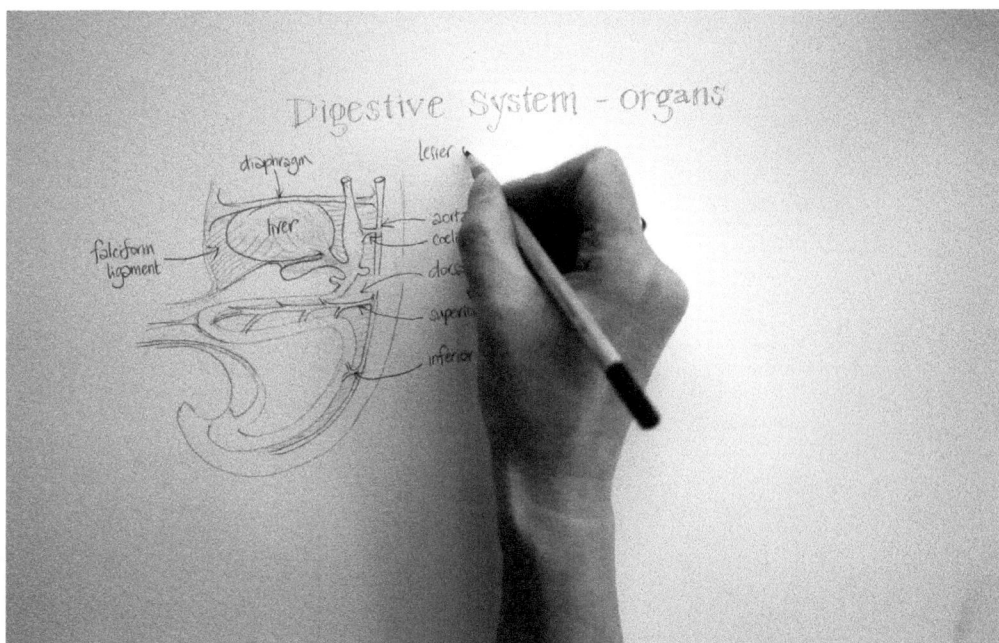

Image used by kind permission of Professor Alice Roberts.

And my first SSAD drawing turned out like this:

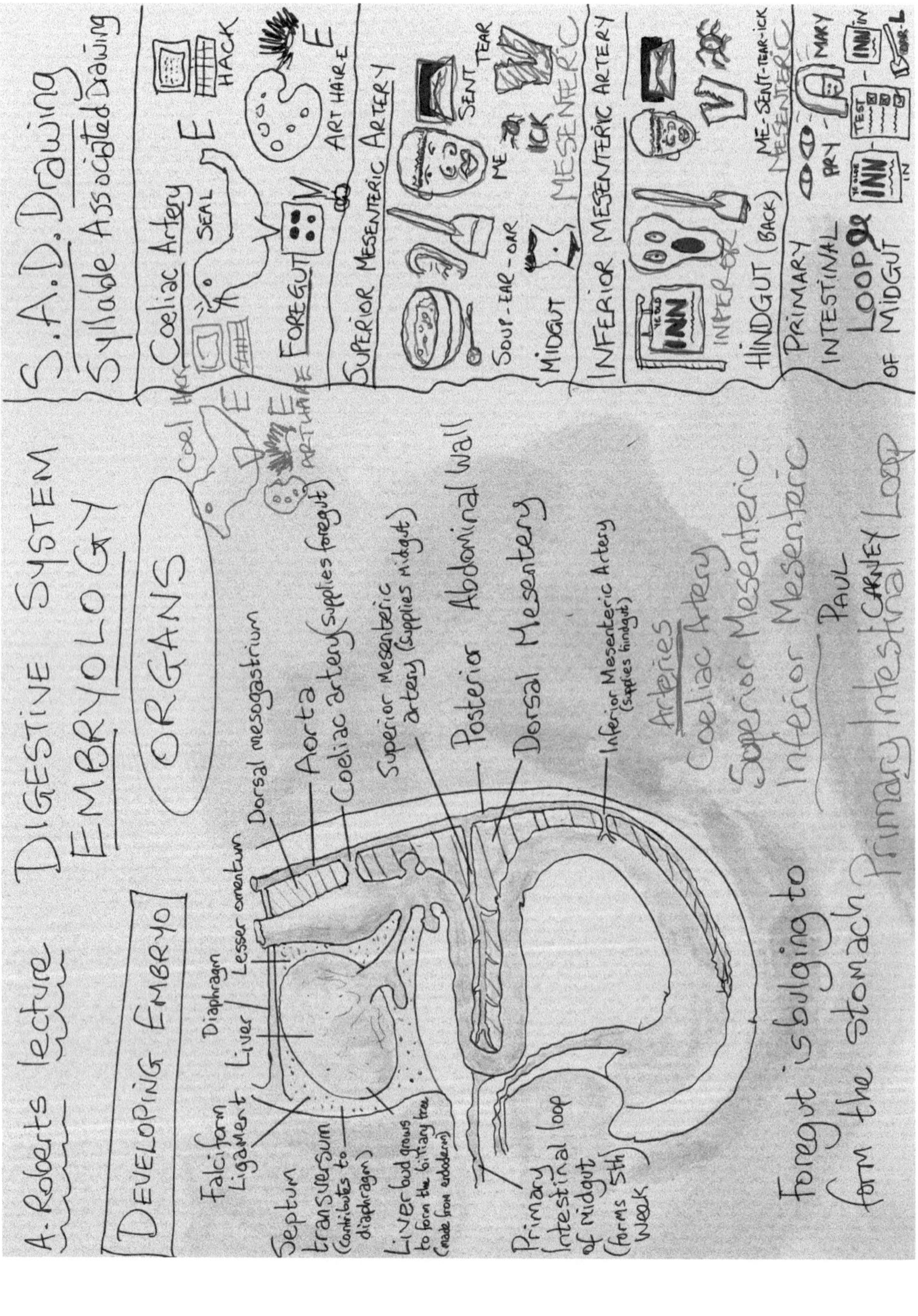

I repeated the drawing at intervals of one hour, one day, one week, one month and I did not need to use this information for any purpose, so it was as close to blind recall as I could get it.

This is my one day drawing. I got the diagram correct, but had struggled to recall three of the key words.

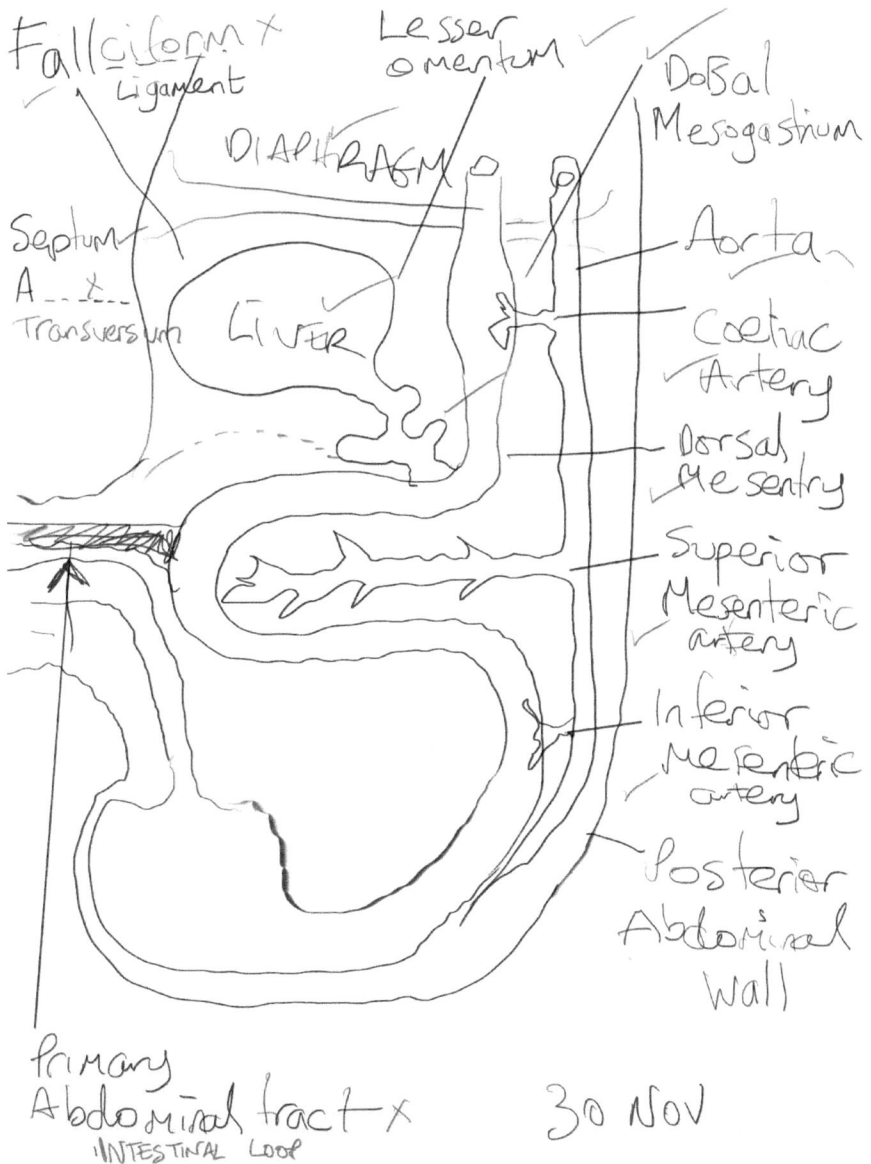

Falciform ✗
Ligament

Lesser
omentum ✓

Dorsal
Mesogastrium

DIAPHRAGM

Septum
A__✗__
Transversum

Liver

Aorta

Coeliac
Artery

Dorsal
Mesentry

Superior
Mesenteric
artery

Inferior
Mesenteric
artery

Posterior
Abdominal
Wall

Primary
Abdominal tract ✗
INTESTINAL LOOP

30 Nov

This is my one week drawing. Some of the drawing was slightly incorrect, but I only forgot one word.

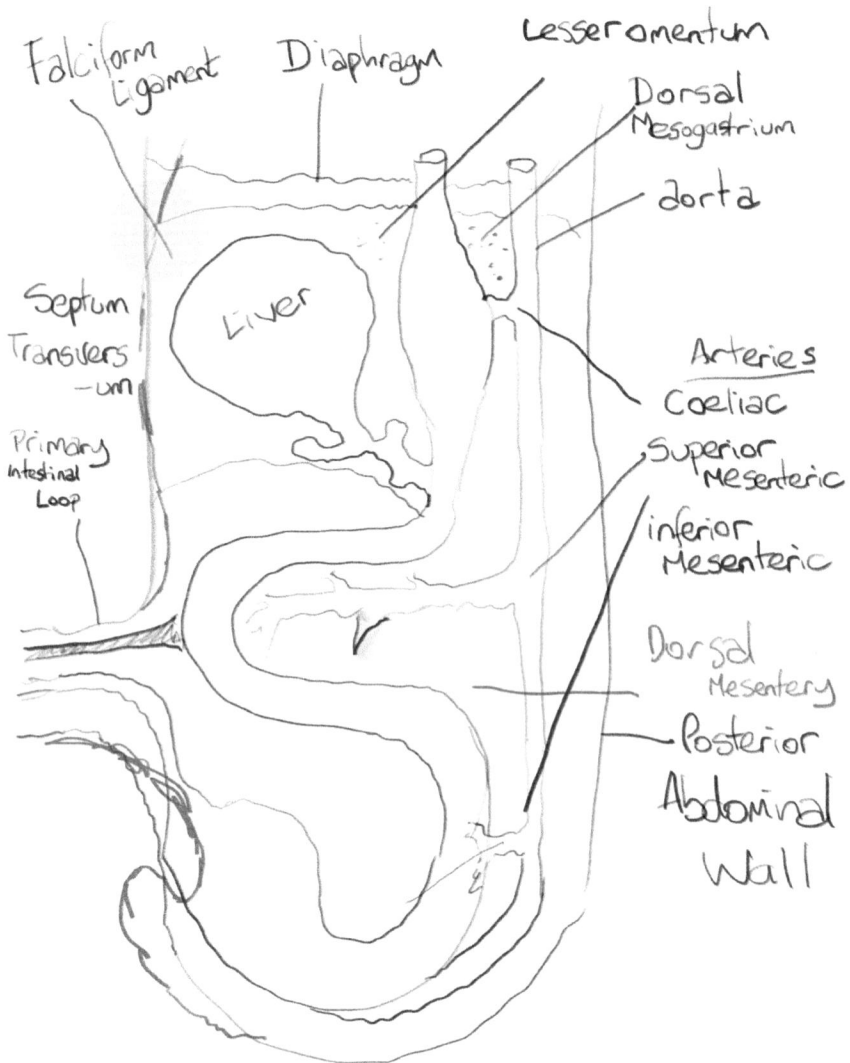

All in all I'm really pleased with the results. I would consider myself to have a really poor memory for names, so this was a huge improvement. I think it is fair to say this shows that the SSAD method really improves memory recall. My advice is to make sure you redraw the visual mnemonics each time, don't skip doing them, because when you are trying to recall the information you need to have that strong mental anchor associated with it.

And finally…

Try taking photos of key notes and organising them into folders on your phone or tablet. I use this technique a lot to remember large amounts of information, but you must not rely on it too much because you get lazy. Only use the photos to refer back to when you are really stuck. In a class situation where phones are not allowed, you might take photos of important notes on a camera then upload them into your own personal storage area on your school shared drive.

Having important notes on your phone means you can refer back to them on the bus home, or when you are writing an assignment, without having to look through lots of old books. Make sure you organise them into folders though!

4. DRAWING FOR UNDERSTANDING
How drawing might help us break down and understand complex meaning in text

Drawing Complex Text 1: Detecting dark matter

We are often asked to read complex text then summarise it or paraphrase it in our own words, to ensure that we have understood it and can remember it. As an illustrator of books, I am often asked to produce illustrations for a writer's texts and this involves me having to paraphrase texts visually. I need to conjure up visualisations from the text, ones that highlight certain aspects or meanings, then draft drawings and artwork from my ideas. Often this process is a collaboration between myself and the writer or publisher, where they instruct me on what it is they want visualising. So how do I turn complex text into a drawing?

Well, you need to be aware of what it is the author is saying and that means reading it and trying to understand it. Then you need to be sure of what the big picture is, what the important lessons are that you need to learn from it. Usually a teacher helps you with this, guiding you and supporting you to understand it. Next, you need to be aware of what type of text it is. There are different types of text such as narrative text, expository text, technical or persuasive text.

These four types of text require us to write in different ways and also to draw in different ways. We might be more imaginative with our drawings when illustrating narrative or persuasive text, but when we are illustrating technical or expository text we usually have to draw exactly what the writer intended.

Whenever you are asked to paraphrase a piece of text or write a summary of it, you will probably read it over a few times. As you are doing that you will almost certainly construct images in your mind of what you are reading. For most of us, these internal mental images aren't like pictures we see on the TV, but rather they are more like a familiarity of an object that we associate with things we know. For example, I might be reading a text describing a bird and in my head I'll be remembering what feathers look like, the shapes and feel of bird's beaks, or the sounds they make and the way they move.

Some people can scan things really quickly and make sense of it. Sometimes however, they are too quick for their own good and they need to slow down, take their time over what they are studying and fully digest it. Drawing helps all of us savour what we are studying, it helps encode and embed the information and make it more concrete.

Take for example this piece of expository text:

> 1,100 metres beneath the earth's surface, in Boulby Underground Laboratory, North Yorkshire, England, over 70 scientists from Universities around the world search for the mysterious Dark Matter that is thought to make up ninety percent of matter in our universe. Boulby is a quiet place, where studies are carried out free of interference from the earth's surface noise, cosmic rays and background radiation. To locate the Dark Matter, the scientists use a device called DRIFT to locate the faint breath of particle winds blowing from a constellation called Cygnus, the Swan, which is many light years from earth.

If I read this text a few times I can work out the key facts: 1100 metres below ground, Boulby Underground Laboratory, North Yorkshire, 70 scientists looking for evidence of dark matter that makes up the universe, free from disturbances, DRIFT machine, breath of a particle wind, Cygnus the swan, distant galaxy.

To draw this text, I first sketched out those key facts in rough form. I actually drew it three times before I got it right. Then I went over it in black pen. This is what I did:

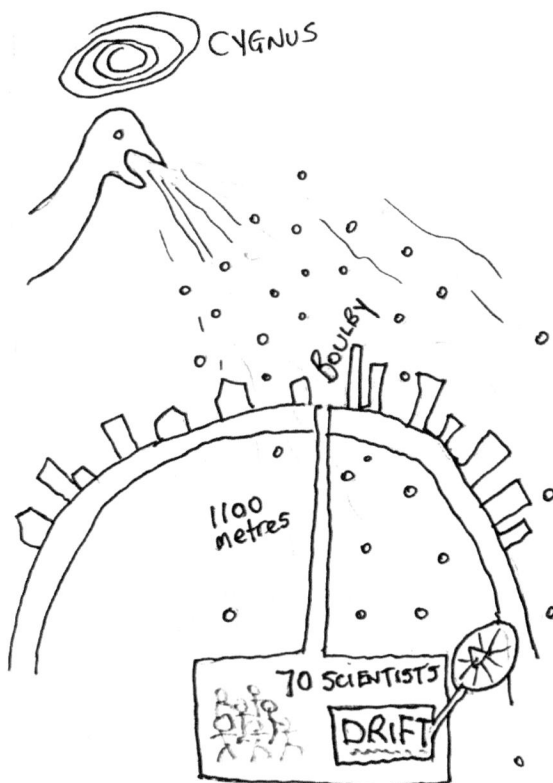

My drawing of the text wasn't beautifully drawn or coloured. It wasn't a work of art, it just illustrated what I needed it to. My swan looks poor, but that's ok.

Notice I drew a swan to represent the galaxy Cygnus and I drew it breathing the particle wind out across space. This powerful image really helps me remember the overall picture of what is happening. Remember though, there isn't only one way to represent this because ANY way you draw it will help you to learn it better.

I can tell you from experience what the strengths and the weaknesses of this method are. Over time, I will remember the swan breathing particles and the lab underground catching them. But I'll struggle to remember key words such as Cygnus, DRIFT, Boulby, 1100 metres, 70 scientists and dark matter because they are more complex and they are only written, not drawn. So I have added some SSAD drawings specifically to remember the key information, using techniques from the previous chapter.

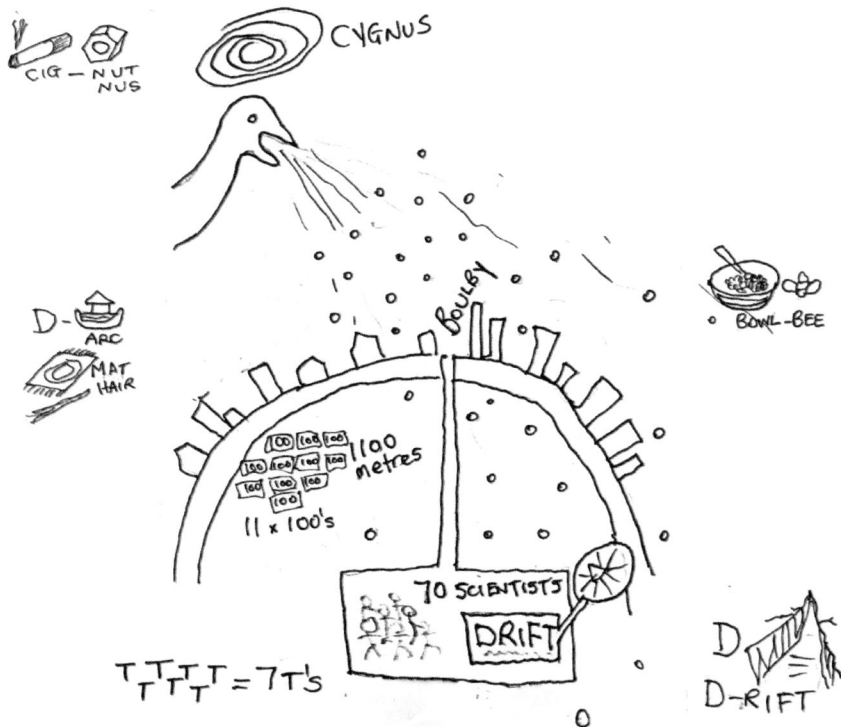

I've added the extra drawings of the fact words and tried to set them out with plenty of space around them so I don't get confused.

Drawing Complex Text 2: To Kill a Mockingbird

Hopefully, you begin to see how drawing complex text can help us understand it better. You might already be used to doing illustrations for text you are studying. I'm not saying I invented the method after all. One way of drawing you might be used to is producing comic strips of stories or plays you are learning. This brilliant method can help you to remember plots and narratives of texts, but we can take this one step further by using the method to help us when we are asked to break down complex texts in English or history. Often in these subjects you are given a piece of text with deeper meanings that aren't easily understood. Drawing can help us here again. For example, take a look at this piece of text from To Kill a Mocking Bird by Harper Lee. This text was the subject of a blog post by English expert Doug Lemov about close reading. I've tried to show how drawing can really help you dissect text like this and make comprehension easier.

"Somewhere, I had received the impression that Fine Folks were people who did the best they could with the sense they had, but Aunt Alexandra was of the opinion, obliquely expressed, that the longer a family had been squatting on one patch of land the finer it was."

The first thing I did was to read it a few times. Then I underlined the key words and phrases in the sentence.

"<u>Somewhere</u>, I had <u>received</u> the <u>impression</u> that <u>Fine Folks</u> were people who <u>did the best they could</u> with the <u>sense they had</u>, but <u>Aunt Alexandra</u> was of the opinion, <u>obliquely expressed</u>, that the <u>longer a family had been squatting</u> on <u>one patch of land</u> the <u>finer it was</u>."

Next, I began drawing all the words I'd underlined. Remember, it doesn't matter how good or bad the drawings are, only that they help you visualise what you are reading. I kept drawing until I'd finished the whole sentence.

After underlining key words and phrases we can draw each one in turn to help us understand.

I have drawn them in a loose comic strip style, keeping the drawings in a neat line above my key words.

I can now more easily see that the sentence is all about Fine Folks and that there are two opinions about what this means. I've separated these opinions as I drew and put them on different lines, like a loose comic strip. I can also see that the narrator (Scout) thinks that these Fine Folks are being kind and doing their best, but Aunt Alexandra thinks that they just have to squat on the land longer, regardless of how good they are.

The way this method works is that it helps you to turn those vague mental ideas into firm pictures on paper. This process of physically drawing your thoughts is a really great learning tool and is something our species have done for millions of years. It can help you to learn regardless of how well you can draw or how clever you are.

Now you might have already understood all of this without going through the whole drawing process. I don't want to make work for you, so if you can do that then great, but remember that drawing deliberately slows you down, it makes you take time over things so you can learn them properly. The danger with rushing ahead is that you forget it as fast as you learn it. If it is important, give it some study time.

This particular exercise has an extra stage to it however and one that requires me to answer some deep questions. (I didn't think of these, they came from Doug's blog and your teacher would ask you them.) I've used a simple comic strip layout and drawn boxes around the key questions for me to write my answers. What this is doing is helping to divide my thinking up, to give my questions some space and help me to focus. Next, I've written some rough notes for my answers. (I'm not saying they are correct!)

FINE PEOPLE DO BEST WITH WHAT THEY HAVE

V.

(kind, wise)

FINE PEOPLE COME FROM TIME ON LAND

KEY QUESTIONS

ANALYSE THIS:

OBLIQUELY EXPRESSED

Sounds nasty, cruel

Dictionary: "done in a direct way."

Snooty
Snobby
Putting poor people down

SQUATTING?

Your family history on the land makes you wealthy.
Breeding, reputation, history.

Why is Fine Folks capitalised?
She thinks fine Folks are very important,
more important than Common people.

I've now written my notes in the boxes to help me frame the questions more clearly.

Drawing Complex Text 3: The Tempest

Let's look at another example of drawing to understand the meaning of complex text, using this verse from Ferdinand in Shakespeare's The Tempest:

"There be some sports are painful, and their labour
Delight in them sets off: some kinds of baseness
Are nobly undergone and most poor matters
Point to rich ends. This my mean task
Would be as heavy to me as odious, but
The mistress which I serve quickens what's dead
And makes my labours pleasures."

The verse goes on to describe his lover Miranda's crabby father and how she weeps as he stacks thousands of logs, yet none of this bothers him because his love carries him through his suffering. For the purposes of this however, I will just focus on what I've written above.

First I read it through a few times. Do I understand what it is saying? What words confuse me? (Sports. Does he mean football or something else?) I use a dictionary to look up the words baseness and odious. When I've done that I think I've worked out that he is saying that he will endure any kind of pain for the woman he loves.

Does that mean I can just move on, without drawing anything? Er, yes if it isn't important that you remember it and don't want to understand it more deeply. In an education setting you are likely to have a teacher who will point to key texts that are important to understand more fully. (You may think the text they are focussing on is dull but that doesn't matter. They are showing you how to study text closely so you can apply it anywhere.)

I don't have a teacher, so I've gone to a website about this text and learned that in Shakespeare's plot, Ferdinand is banished to an island for twelve years by Miranda's evil father Prospero. So I simply sketch out in rough the key parts of the text.

sports are painful, and their labour Delight in them

some kinds of baseness Are nobly undergone

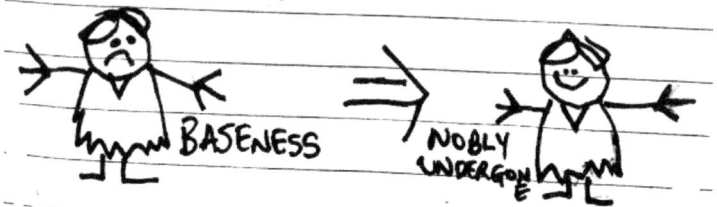

most poor matters Point to rich ends.

This my mean task Would be as heavy to me as odious, but The mistress which I serve quickens what's dead And makes my labours pleasures

But these are only my sketches. I need to check I've got things right. You may need to check it with a teacher, but I have read more notes about the play and realised I've done some things wrong. Ferdinand was made to move logs not dig on an island. And I missed out 'quickens what's dead'. I also need to make Ferdinand's love for Miranda more central to the drawing, after all this is the focus of the whole speech. So I re-drew my drawing and, rightly or wrongly, I omitted Prospero, because I didn't feel he was important to this part of the speech. This is what I drew:

This is my third drawing of this text and my drawing skills have improved each time. Each time I'm trying to make it clearer, less cluttered.

The point of this drawing is that it helps you to visualise the speech, to create more vivid mental images of Ferdinand's love for Miranda, and it helps you to fully understand the true depth of his love for her. When you are asked to answer questions about this passage, you will remember your little sketches and they will help you to write more eloquently about it.

Drawing to understand complex plots 1: Midsummer Night's Dream

When you need to learn a play or a book you should spend some time learning the plot of the book and its characters. You need the facts of the book firmly established before you can begin studying it in more depth. Sometimes we only use a text-based list or a written plot summary, but remember we now know that people learn more effectively when they draw information rather than write it.

One excellent way of drawing complex plots is through the comic strip, where stages of the plot are divided into boxes and we use a combination of pictures and text to understand it. I wanted to study Midsummer Night's Dream by William Shakespeare so I read the plot first, then drew it as a rough comic strip using drawings and text.

This is too cluttered; there's too much text and it is confusing. It has however, helped me understand it better, but I just need to do it again with more drawing.

This method helped a lot. This play has a very complex storyline and is very confusing. You need to go over this plot a few more times, you need to spend time learning the characters and processing the information. Think back to our pizza delivery guy. After I've drawn the comic strip, the information has become like that single track road, bumpy and hard to navigate. If we want to make it into a super-highway, we need to spend more time building those brain cell connections. I need to do some more drawing. Firstly, I want to draw the characters again and learn their names.

My next drawings have separated the story characters from their names, that I've drawn using my memory technique. This is much clearer than my last effort!

This extra time spent drawing the characters and names helped me a lot to remember them. It slowed me down, made me spend more time with the new words, I broke them up into syllables and made visual associations with the sounds, using my SSAD technique. I will probably forget the names again, but whenever I do I can look back at my drawings and re-associate the drawings, such as a hippo and a lighter for Hippolyta.

This isn't the end of our plot studies though; it is only the beginning. Now I need to draw more pictures for each section of my comic strip, such as who loves who in this confusing tale!

So how do I solve this? Easy, I just draw my characters again and use arrows and hearts to indicate who loves who.

Lysander and Hermia love each other. Helena loves Dimitrius but he loves Hermia.

Now I need to do this with every other section of the plot! I know, it takes time, but that is precisely how and why you will learn and remember it. Here is my example drawing of another section of the plot. I have now drawn these characters three or four times, but I really enjoyed doing it.

My drawing style is still rough, but it is helping me slowly encode the information I need to learn.

Drawing to understand complex plots 2: Henry the Fifth

We can take this method even further by eliminating text almost completely. Here is a famous historic play produced by drawing. Can you 'read' the drawing and understand what is happening?

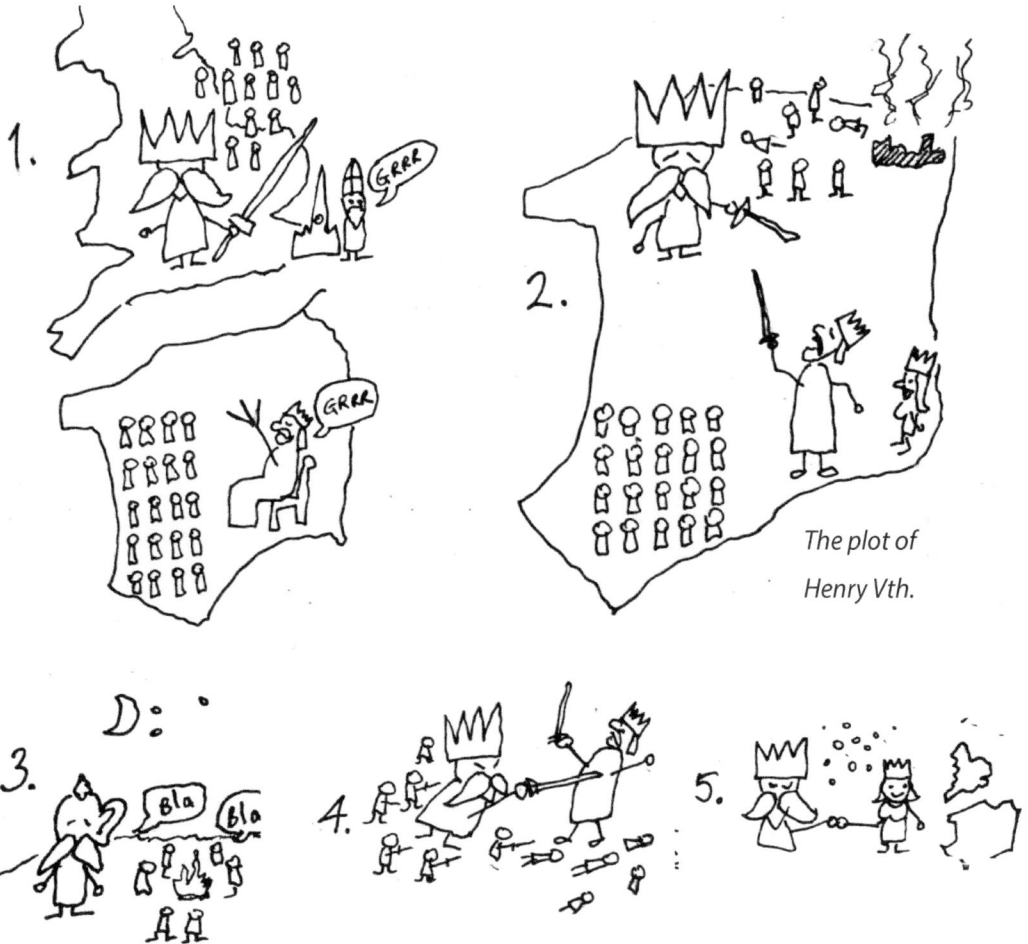

The plot of Henry Vth.

1. The English king is looking toward France, his army behind him, his sword raised. A church leader angrily warns him. The French king has a bigger army, he is seated to symbolise his power, but he raises his hand to stop the English king.

2. The English king has invaded France but met strong resistance in the north. His army looks defeated. The French king raises his sword, his army is strong and he stands in front of a girl, maybe a queen or a princess.

3. We can just make out this is the king from his moustache, though he does not wear his crown. He is in disguise, standing next to some men and listening to their conversations.

4. The English king is piercing the chest of the French king in battle. Against all odds, he has won.

5. The English king is now holding the hand of the queen/princess from the earlier picture. They are getting married and the maps of England and France are shown to symbolise that they are now united.

This is the story of William Shakespeare's play Henry the Fifth. It is drawn with a technique that was used for centuries to tell stories, before people could read. It was used in the Bayeux Tapestry and in most Western paintings. This is difficult, but if you can do this you are really drawing for learning.

These are my rough initial notes and sketches from the synopsis I read of Henry the Fifth.

I wanted to show you the thinking process behind the drawing. A lot of thinking, planning and refinement of information takes place to create a simple picture.

Using drawing to understand essay questions

It is often the case in academic learning that a key or essential question is posed as the starting point for a discussion or an essay. Students must pick apart the question then attempt to answer it in the form of a discussion, an essay or a short paragraph. Usually this requires the learner to possess a complex level of language in order to understand the question and answer it properly. It also requires the student to know the rules and conventions of how to answer such complex questions.

Now there are many excellent students who probably will not need to perform drawing exercises in order to understand a complex question. I accept that, but drawing slows you down, makes you digest information and makes you process it correctly.

Let us now look at an essay question from a history lesson and try to use drawing to help us visualise and understand it better.

'Describe the factors that led to the end of the Bronze Age in the Ancient Middle East.'

This is a complicated question to answer, so let's break it down by sentence structure. Sentences have three main parts: a subject that is performing an action, an object (direct or indirect) that receives the action, and a predicate that expresses this action.

1. Describe the factors. This is the sentence subject but I'm unsure about this, I don't know what they are.

2. End of the Bronze Age. This is an action or event in time so it must be the predicate of the sentence.

3. Ancient Middle East. This is the object of the sentence because the question is asking us to describe events that took place here.

So I now know that something unknown is causing the Bronze Age to end in the Ancient Middle East. Let's try to visualise through drawing what it is I'm writing about. I can do a simple image search in a web browser or use an encyclopaedia to search the terms: Bronze Age and Ancient Middle East. I check and verify my results first to make sure they are correct and make quick drawings of what stands out. I must say firstly, that I got a lot of results and I was very confused about what was relevant to my question and what wasn't, so you may need to check with a teacher that you are correct before you draw anything. However, I then copied my pictures roughly:

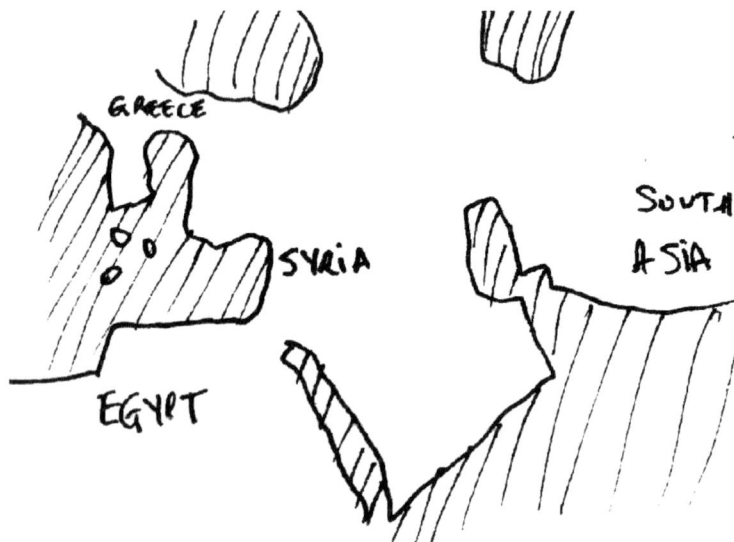

Here is my sketch of a map of the Ancient Middle East. I had to check that this was from the right time because the place names have changed a lot since then.

What my drawings have revealed is where the Ancient Middle East was and what the people probably looked like. I can see that people wore clothes but that men wore skirt-like garments and boots. I can see people lived in small houses without windows, they rode horses, they fought mainly with spears and shields and they lived quite simply compared to modern standards. I found out that there were lots of different styles of buildings, clothes and armour according to where you were from. I found out that late Bronze Age armour and weaponry were more advanced than early Bronze Age ones.

Drawings of late Bronze Age people.

If I was coming to this question without any prior knowledge of the Ancient Middle East and the Bronze Age, I have learned a lot from just doing this exercise. An important learning phase was achieved through me having to find my own pictures and decide which were correct and which weren't. If a teacher only gives you the correct pictures then an important learning aspect is missed out, because by forcing me to select only the right ones, I'm seeing how they are different.

This works with the map too, because in modern maps there are countries in those places that weren't there in the Ancient Middle East such as Saudi Arabia. I got a few pictures wrong (I don't think those roofs are correct for the Middle East in my drawing for example) but the process of getting stuff wrong then putting it right helps you learn. What's most important though is that I now have a better understanding of the context of the question. I know where and when this question is set, and can visualise better what the people looked like.

I now research the causes for the Bronze Age collapse and find that over a fifty year period between 1250-1150 BCE almost every major city in the Ancient Middle East fell into ruin. The causes of this collapse are believed to have been:

Earthquakes, drought & famine, war, invasion by sea peoples, political conflict, trade collapse.

Simple sketches of the causes of the Bronze Age collapse, quickly copied from internet clip art.

I simply did an internet image search for each one of the things I'd found in my research then typed 'earthquake drawings' or 'drought drawings' and on a few occasions I added 'Ancient Middle East' or 'Ancient Greece'. I picked the simplest ones I could because I'm not trying to do a beautiful, intricate drawing. This is an essay not an art lesson. What I've done so far has given me a strong visual outline of the essay question. I can see the scene in my mind more clearly, it feels more familiar to me now.

What's more, I have a better chance of remembering those six factors that led to the collapse of the Ancient Middle East in the Bronze Age than if I'd just written them out, because drawing helps me remember them.

The main essay types. The person in the argumentative response is supposed to be pleading! It's not a good drawing but I left it in to show you that your own drawings don't have to be perfect.

My method might seem a little child-like to you. You might be tempted to think it is suitable only for less able or younger students, but I can assure you that drawing written information at any academic level will not only help you remember stuff more effectively, but it will help you understand it more easily. If you're stuck on something – draw it!

There are of course different ways of writing essays; critical, argumentative, comparison, narrative. A good lesson activity is to try to illustrate these four essay types using only drawing. You can use diagrams now to plan out your essay, following the type of approach you are using to answer this question. It doesn't have to be achingly beautiful or done on a computer, just sketch it out in rough, but it should be done by you, not a handout from a teacher.

A quick diagram of my essay structure. I can rub out and refine my statements if I need to. Don't waste time making it look beautiful, it is a working diagram.

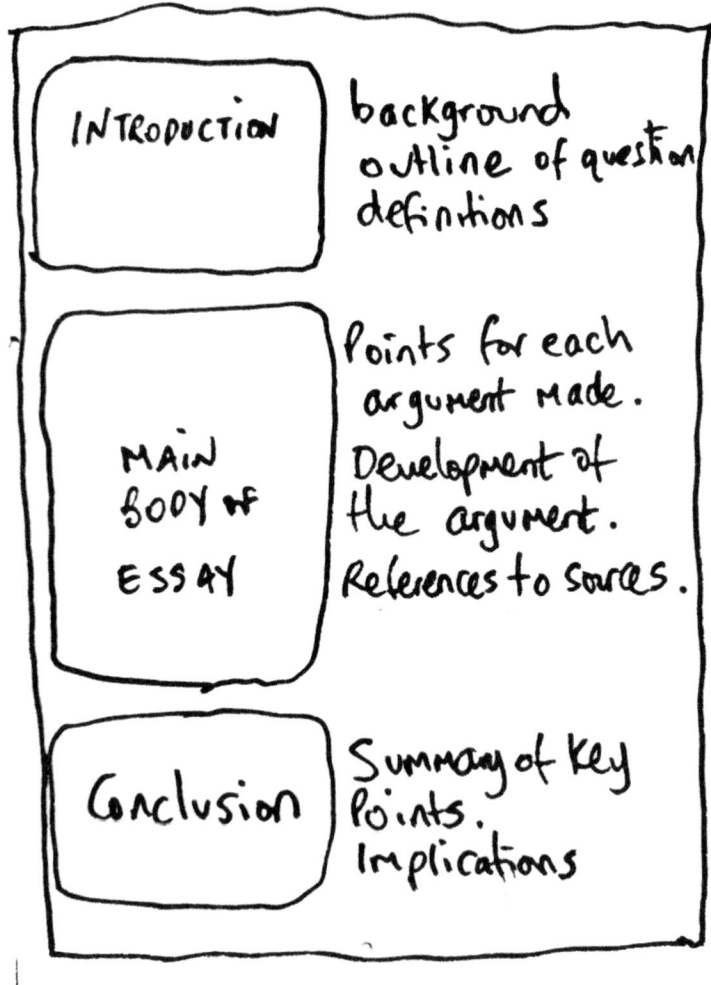

INTRODUCTION

background
outline of question
definitions

MAIN
BODY of
ESSAY

Points for each
argument made.
Development of
the argument.
References to sources.

Conclusion

Summary of key
points.
Implications

Narrative drawing: Drawing information without text

We have crossed a threshold in our understanding of drawing for learning, because we have now used visual imagery in a way that isn't used often today. Remember, most of the general population weren't able to read and write a hundred years ago. Pictures were a significant way to tell stories and transmit information. Images weren't an outlier to the writing, a piece of decoration or an afterthought, they were a principle method of telling people what had happened. What good were history books if few could read them?

This is what the Bayeux Tapestry was, and also the Codex Zouche-Nuttall, a Mexican pictograph book produced in the 14th century by the Mixtec people to record their conquests and their ancestors. People used drawing at a very sophisticated level to tell a whole story, without words.

The Bayeux Tapestry requires us to study it very closely if we are to understand its message and even then, we know it was written by the victor and so it might not be entirely accurate.

But we can still use this technique today, especially since we now know how much more we remember by drawing rather than writing. We might employ these narrative drawing techniques during a language lesson to create a scene of an event in a café, restaurant or shop that must then be translated into a different language. We might use narrative drawing to remind us of a sequence or process we need to solve an equation or a formula. We might use it to describe a significant historical event, person or artist. It could even be used as instruction for a sporting technique.

This style of drawing is usually done for us, prior to learning, by professional illustrators, but if we are challenged to do the illustrating of the plain text ourselves, we will usually learn it better.

Book illustrations and designs are beautiful, but they often give us everything on a plate, they set information out neatly, colour it and design it, then add all the pictures and photographs for us. This has many advantages of course. It would be really dull if we just had to learn from pages and pages of plain text (although we do it when we read books!). The disadvantage of this is the person who has received the most amount of learning from the topic is the illustrator who drew the pictures. What I'm saying is that you, the reader, need to go through this process if you are to learn better. We all need to be illustrators, ones that don't even need to be able to draw, because doing it helps us learn better.

Let me show you an example of illustrating text for learning. I will try to show you how I answered the question: 'What factors led to the Battle of Hastings in 1066? Who were the main claimants to the throne?'

The first thing I did was to read information about this event from reliable sources a few times so I had understood it. I tried to avoid looking at other people's sources of visual information, because I wanted to form my own impressions of what things should look like. If I see too many pictures it makes me want to copy them accurately and my own imagination suffers.

When I was sure I knew what had happened I began drawing. I needed to show who had died, why this was important, who the main claimants to the throne were and where they were from. I copied a map of Europe (really badly) and drew characters from the Bayeux Tapestry, though I just made up my little soldiers. I thought about how I would answer the question, without worrying about how good or bad my drawings were.

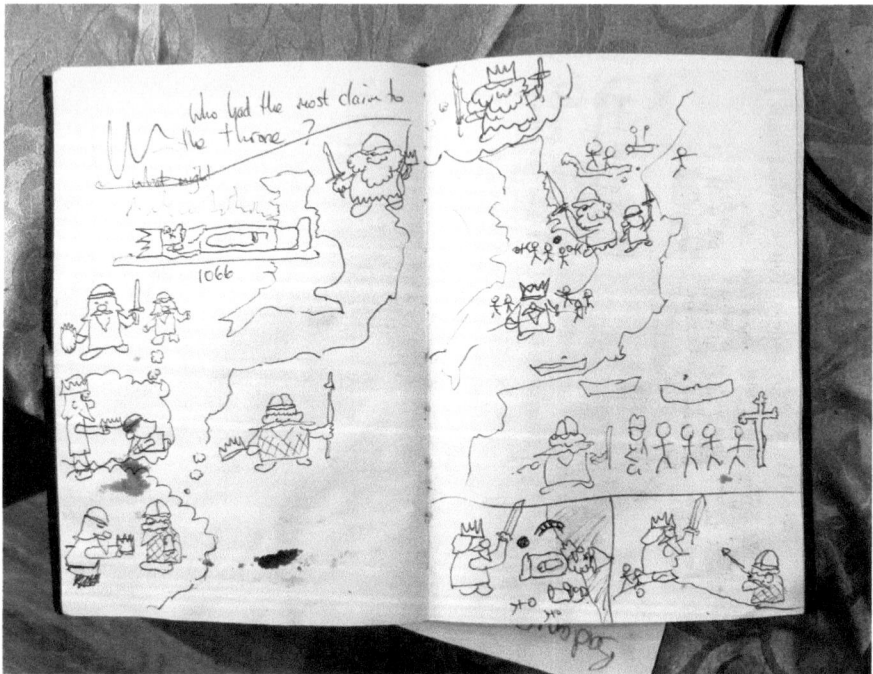

These are my sketchbook pages trying to work out what I needed to show in my answer and how to do that best.

When I was satisfied, I checked my answers, then sketched out a final idea in rough, before going over it again in black pen. I wanted my drawing to answer the question without using any text, so that the viewer would have to 'read' the picture.

In my example, you can see that I've drawn the dead king Edward, I've drawn the Anglo-Saxon king Harold holding up the crown and added a smaller figure behind him to represent his brother Tostig who is holding a knife at his back. Harald Hardrada in Norway and William Duke of Normandy in France both hold up crowns also. The only text I've added is the date.

You should be able to read a whole story from this drawing,
even if you have never heard of the Battle of Hastings.

This drawing tells us a lot about the factors that led to the Battle of Hastings but I am not trying to say that it is all you need to do to answer the question I posed. We would now need to go on to write a detailed account of the factors that led to the battle, the names of the characters, their beliefs about their claim etc. The important thing here though is that the drawing has come first, before the writing. I've used drawing to lead me into the more complicated stuff, and in doing so I've actually understood it better than if I had simply read it in a text book .

If I'd simply copied this picture from a book it wouldn't be as effective, because to learn it, I need to go through the process of piecing the picture together, getting it wrong, redrawing it, adding things, taking things away. Even if all I'd drawn were stick people I'd still know a lot more about where these key players were from than if I'd just read it in a book, because the visual process of drawing it embeds it in my cognition more effectively.

Illustrations and drawings shouldn't just be there to decorate the text we have written, or put there as an afterthought to further explain our writing. Rather, they should come at the beginning to help us to digest and process information so that we understand it better. They are a very powerful means of communication in their own right.

We often don't even need any text to assemble a flat pack piece of furniture. We use illustrated instructions to show us what to do and often rely solely on drawings for information. So drawing is a powerful way to convey meaning. The only barrier we face is one we erect ourselves, in our own minds. We believe that drawing should be accurate and realistic, and we compare ourselves unfairly to people 'better' than us. Then teachers, (who usually have negative beliefs about their own drawing ability) teach us that writing is the most important way to think, and that drawing is largely irrelevant or merely decorative.

I hope I'm beginning to convince you otherwise, because now we are going to draw time.

5. DRAWING IN FOUR DIMENSIONS
Using drawing across time and space to improve metacognition

What is four-dimensional drawing?

When we think of drawing we usually refer to a two-dimensional process on a flat surface using a pencil, pen or other drawing tool. From the time of the Renaissance in the sixteenth century, artists began using visual effects such as perspective and tonal shading to create the illusion of three dimensions on a flat surface. This remained the norm, but then in the early twentieth century, film was invented, and so time began to be represented in films and animations. A movie therefore is a series of two-dimensional images played in such a fast sequence that they appear to move.

Comic strips are a series of events drawn like the cells in an old movie film to represent a story or actions. You can draw time like that, but let me show you how this might be developed further for lessons and learning. Whenever we are shown how to do something, we are shown sequences of learning we must mimic, like the juggler drawings pictured.

I have drawn the sequence of steps you need to go through to learn to juggle.

But the reality of learning to juggle is very different from reading instructions, or even watching a video, because there are a lot of actions the drawing can't show, your failings, your mistakes and errors. What is needed as you learn is a coach to help you, but this isn't often possible. If, however, you drew the actual events of what happened as you tried to learn to juggle, you would formalise your successes and frustrations, and encode your learning process more firmly in your brain. In short, what you're doing by drawing an evaluation of the process of learning is visualising what is usually only articulated internally, or verbally at best. Constant repetition can and does lead us to learning a skill, but many give up out of frustration. Drawing can help to anchor our thoughts and actions, make them more tangible and in doing so, help reduce the time it takes us to learn the new skill and reduce our frustrations. Just saying or thinking your actions isn't always enough. Usually, we know we are doing it wrong, but we don't understand why. If we go back to our juggling analogy, we might use drawing post-mortem to quickly note the flaws in our learning process. You could film yourself learning the skill, and observe your mistakes, this is also effective, but Fernandes et al.'s research in our introduction tells us drawing is more effective for permanent and long-lasting learning.

Now I have drawn my juggling experiences and in doing so I have realised why I keep failing at it and how to remedy it myself.

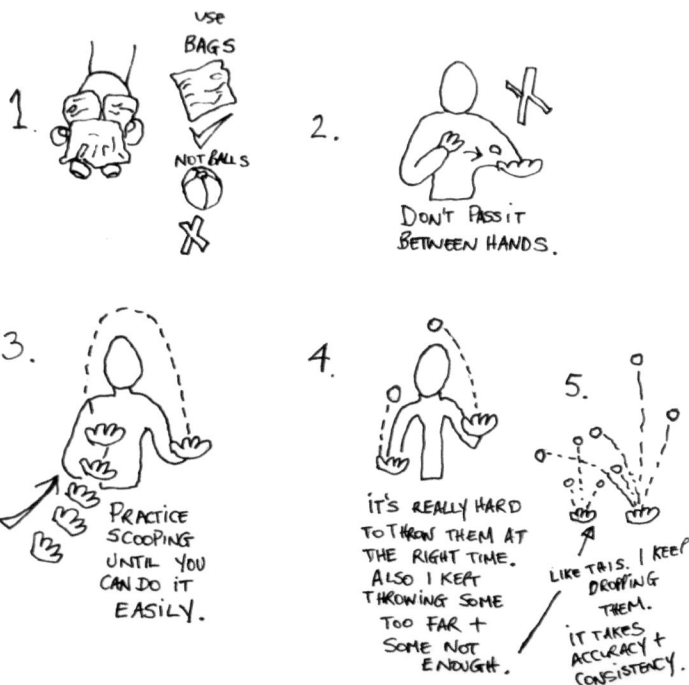

1. USE BAGS NOT BALLS

2. DON'T PASS IT BETWEEN HANDS.

3. PRACTICE SCOOPING UNTIL YOU CAN DO IT EASILY.

4. IT'S REALLY HARD TO THROW THEM AT THE RIGHT TIME. ALSO I KEPT THROWING SOME TOO FAR + SOME NOT ENOUGH.

5. LIKE THIS. I KEEP DROPPING THEM. IT TAKES ACCURACY + CONSISTENCY.

This process of drawing events is an important evaluation technique, and drawing our learning process gets us to visualise what we are doing well and our failings. Think of being handed a DIY flat-pack chest of drawers and a set of instructions. You'd follow the instructions, but if you were then asked to draw over them and record what actually happened as you were assembling it, it might be full of scribbles and angry notes in certain places.

So we have identified a method of how we can use drawing for understanding.

1. Plan your intentions as a series of stages or actions using drawing.

2. Metacognitively evaluate each stage of the learning process as soon as possible after the event.

We can use this technique whenever we are asked to learn a new skill or record a series of actions. For example, in science lessons you are often asked to carry out an experiment. This is usually described for you by a teacher and you are told what the purpose of doing it is, prior to carrying it out as they describe. This is a good first step to learning how to do experiments, but when you become more confident, you should be asked to design your own experiments, and this is where drawing can help you.

You might begin with quick sketches and diagrams, write down important information and then set it up and carry it out. This is good practice, but I think we can go one step further. If we draw a step-by-step series of drawings of the experiment before we begin, we can analyse it more clearly. By drawing it out first we are visualising what is to come, just as an architect draws a plan of a building. This process of visualisation slows us down, makes us consider more fully what we are going to do and spot any potential errors. We might even show this drawing to peers who could evaluate it for us and give us their considered opinion.

What I suggest when doing these preliminary planning drawings, is that you leave large blank spaces between your drawing stages. The large blank spaces will be used to record the process of what actually happened when we performed the experiment, and we can record what happens in real time while it is fresh in our memory. For example, I chose this inertia experiment described on Steve Spangler's brilliant science website, which was described in full text detail with photographic support. I could have proceeded to do the experiment straight away, surely the drawing was a mere distraction. But no, by drawing it I learned more fully what I was being asked to do.

You might draw the initial experiment yourself first,
to make sure you know what to do.

As I did the experiment, I drew diagrams and made notes to record what happened. In this way, drawing serves as an important learning and evaluation tool to enhance metacognitive understanding. We are using drawing to reinforce and support our learning process. These fluid, metacognitive notes and sketches will help us write up our more precise evaluation of our experiment later.

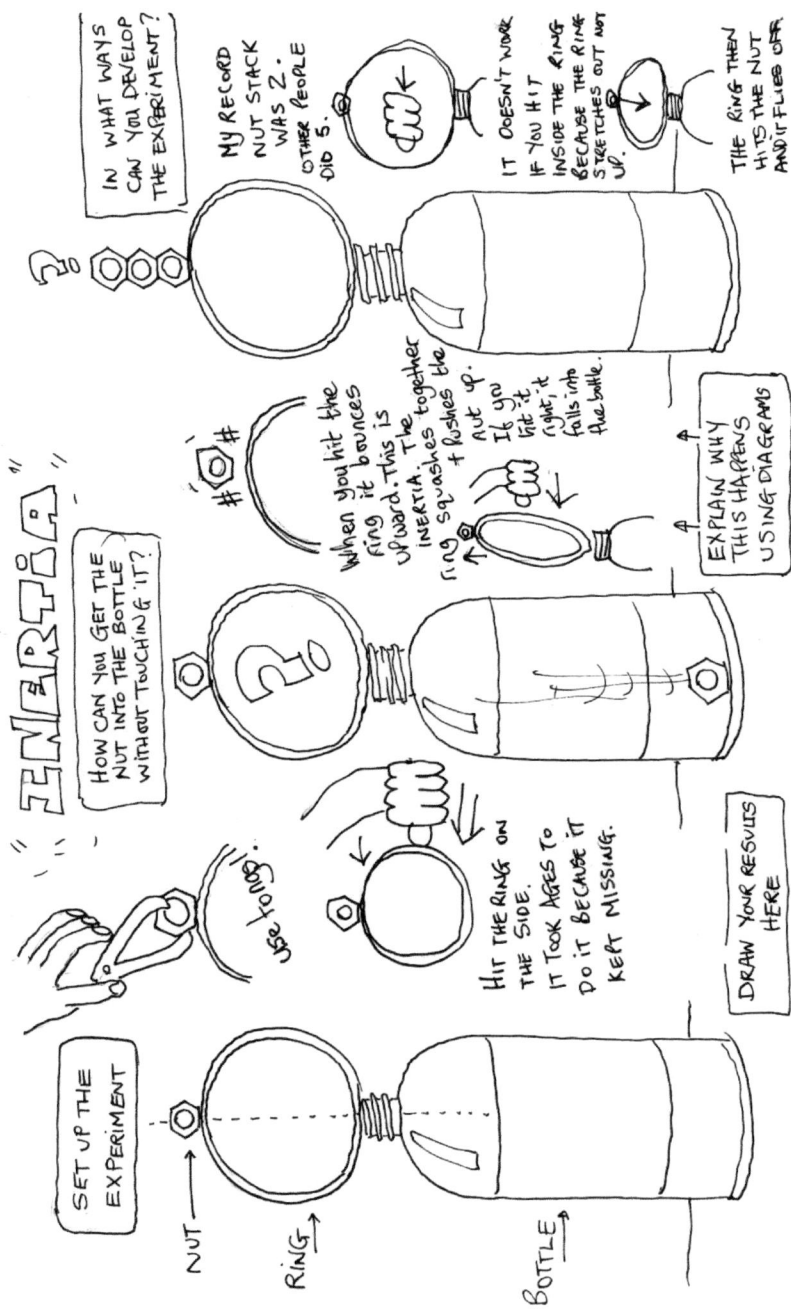

Then review the process through metacognitive drawing.

Drawing is now being used, not as a mere aesthetic, but as a means of organising, planning and visualising our thinking, as well as recording actions and events as they happen in real time.

Applying four-dimensional metacognitive drawing

There is real scope to use this kind of drawing to learn processes in science, or historical events, to play a new musical instrument, to learn stories or dances, or to design and make in Design and Technology. If you want to evaluate or record what took place, you might make lots of written notes or relay them verbally of course, but the most effective way of doing this is drawing the events that actually took place.

For example, the procedure for a total hip replacement could become a visual process that would assist novices to learn the procedure.

If you are put off by the quality of these drawings, don't be. I copied and traced them all from photographs. It took me a long time, tracing, then drawing lightly in pencil first, then going over in black fine liner pen. I also drew them large scale then shrunk them down.

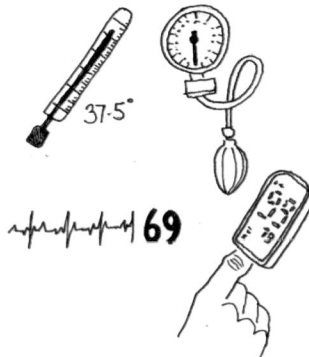

1. Check vital signs.

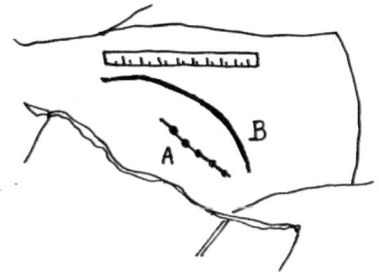

2. Mark patient's hip for surgery.

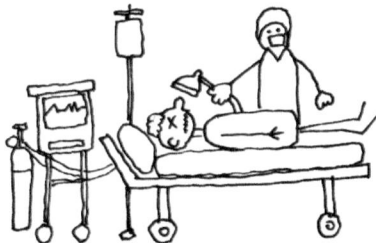

3. Anaesthetic is administered.

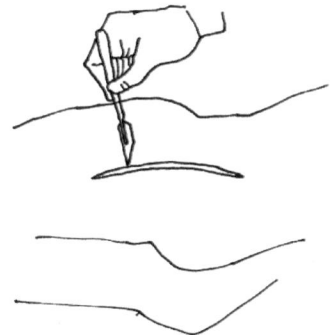

4. The surgeon makes an incision at the side or back of the hip.

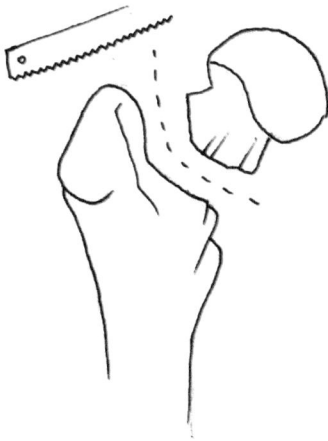

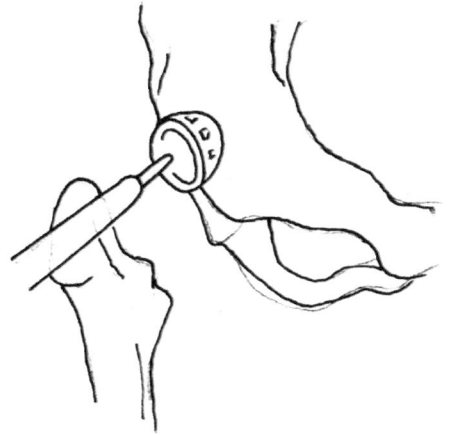

5. The surgeon dislocates the joint from the acetabulum socket in the pelvis. The femoral head is cut off with a bone saw.

6. Use a hemispheric reamer to grind and shape the acetabulum to fit the acetabular prosthetic cup. Place the acetabular cup into the reshaped socket. Fit an insert/liner inside the acetabular cup.

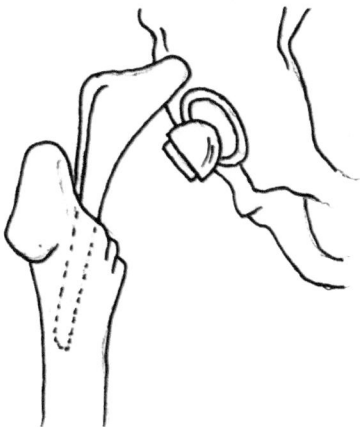

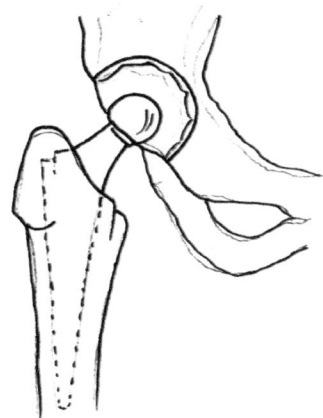

7. Prepare the femur bone and insert the prosthetic femoral stem into it.

8. Fit the prosthetic ball onto the femoral head. Fit the new prosthetic femur into the acetabular cup.

This would assist a novice surgeon, and help them consider and think about each stage of the process they are going to undertake. However, these visual instructions could also be used as an evaluation process after the event, to guide administration staff or other practitioners and so improve future practice.

This format allows the surgeon to make quick evaluations of surgical procedures. The same format could be applied to other fields and processes.

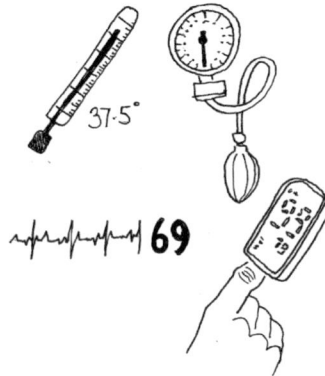

If done over time with multiple people, you can see patterns of where problems are more easily.

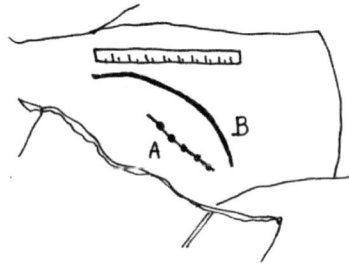

What are the upper + lower levels?
Unsure of tolerances. O^2 slightly raised, other vitals ok.

Surgery Marks had to be re-done. Please see guidance above.

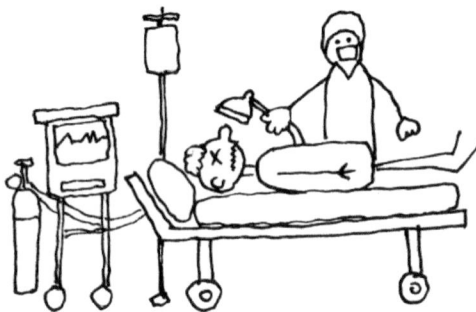

What type of Anethesia? Regional / Spinal, relaxant?

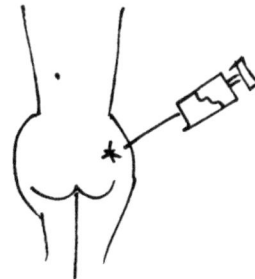

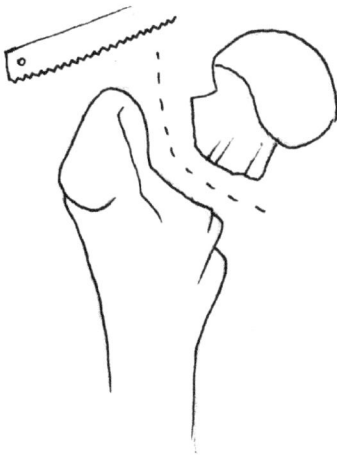

Removing
femur
was
problematic

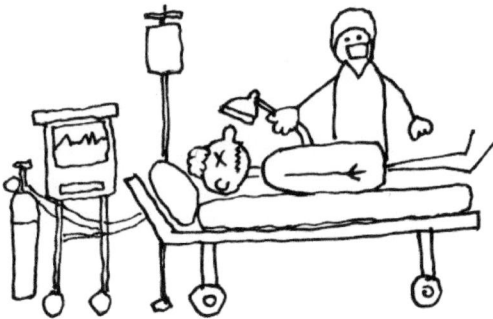

wrong acetabular cup.
use ceramic with
bone cement.

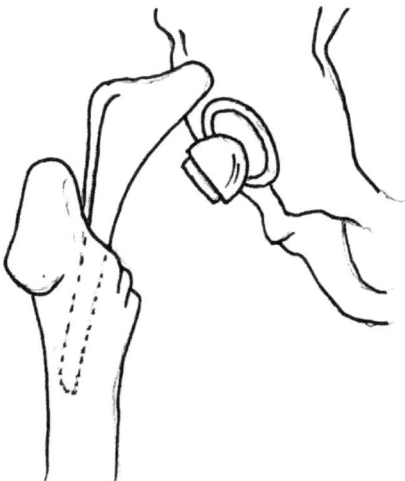

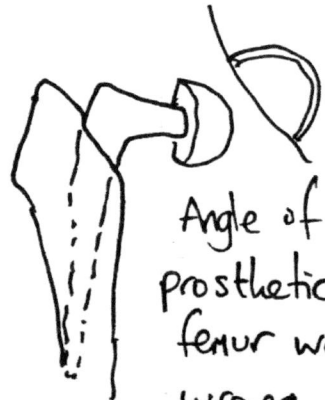

Angle of
prosthetic
femur was
wrong.

We can take our four-dimensional drawing even further and make it more precise if we wish. In the visual example over the next few pages, I have developed my hip operation even further, but this might easily be a time lapse sequence of a volcanic eruption, egg fertilisation, growth of an organism, a life cycle, a golf swing, a high jump or free kick, or a whole host of other events.

I have never performed a hip operation, but my study into how this practice is performed, my drawings of key stages of the operation and evaluation drawings of my subsequent practice has yielded good results.

Also, like any good Ikea instruction manual, I can highlight the tools and instruments I'll need at any stage of the operation. I can add a timeline under my drawing and indicate more precise intervals, moments when I'll need these instruments or even when I desire to give instructions to my team. For example, I could highlight where I want blood pressure or heart rate checking. I can, by giving a copy of this to each of my team, provide them with a detailed plan of how this procedure should unfold. An administrative team might study such plans over time to identify patterns of behaviour, or to spot errors in order to improve efficiency.

The idea of a centralised operation plan, to be given to patients, surgeons, anaesthetists and administration staff alike, is something of a pipe dream in hospitals, where exist huge piles of repetitious paperwork that must cost millions in lost time and also produce many errors. The beauty of the drawing system is that it can be digitised for peanuts, and so exist as a post-operative leaflet to give to patients, or on a tablet as an editable pdf. There is no confusion then about which operation is being done, no struggling to read dodgy handwriting, or uncertainty about the procedure or what to do to aid recovery. You're not battling against language barriers either. Everyone can work on one shared document which serves all purposes and through the simple art of drawing, it can be made possible.

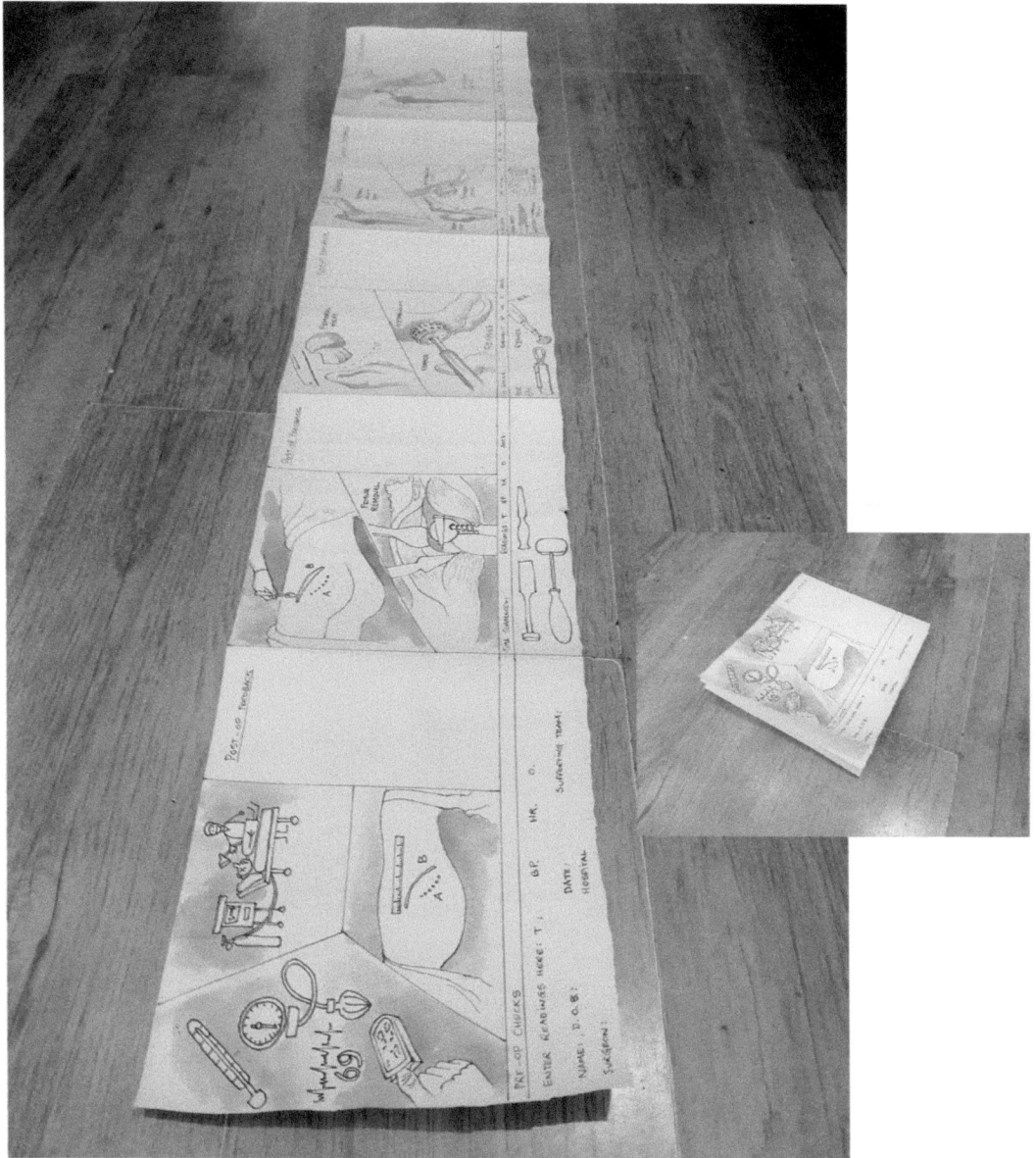

Four-dimensional drawings work well on long strips of paper, folded into a concertina pattern. Each page is then used as a stage of the process being studied. The timeline is drawn in the bottom fifth of the page, and the right margin of each page is kept free for future notes and sketches. See over for more details. This could easily be digitised also.

My 4D drawing of a hip operation in more detail. Hopefully you can see I've split panels into two where I need to conserve space and for efficiency. My drawings may be above what non-skilled artists feel they can achieve, but these might be traced or copied.
It is the process of transferring your inner thoughts to external, visual ideas that matters most, because you learn the process more effectively as you are doing it.

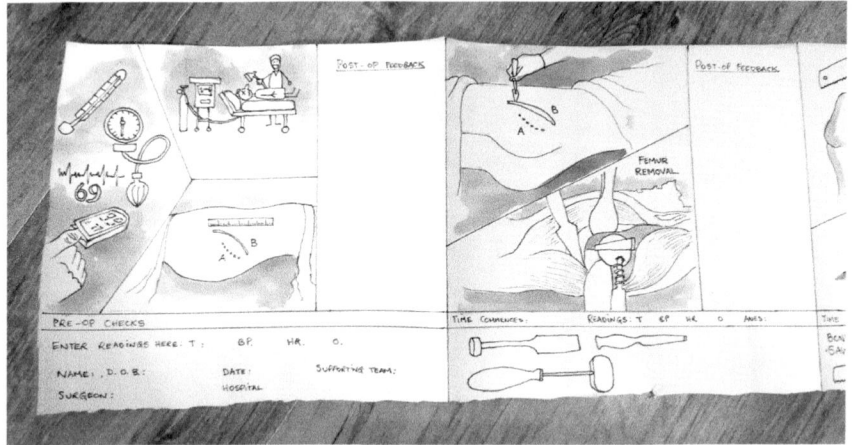

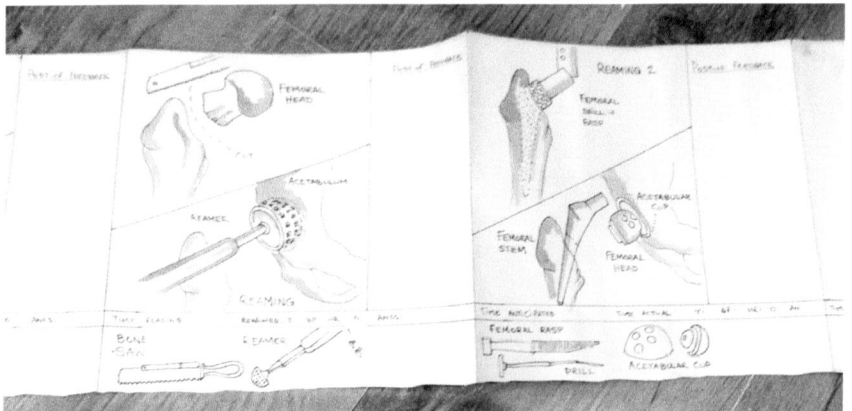

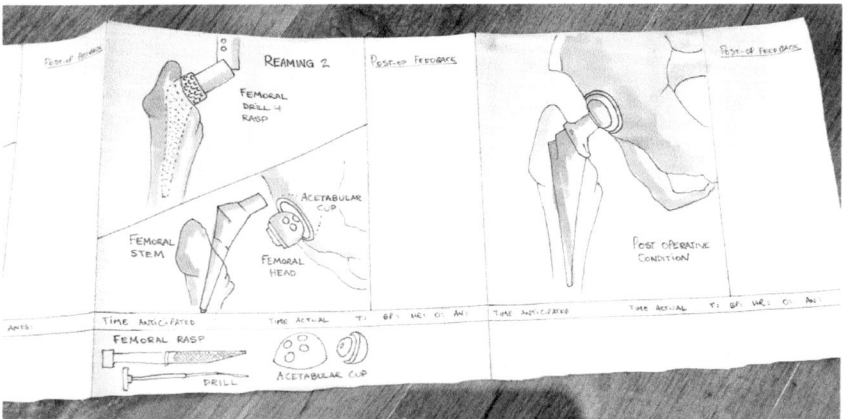

Using my hip operation analogy, the timeline might record hours and minutes. If I was mapping a volcanic eruption, this timeline might record days, weeks or years. If it was a foetus it might display months and days, even hours in places. I could add drawings of influential factors that might occur at key moments, or when processes might diverge into new events. So we can zoom in if we need to or bypass long periods of inactivity.

The first drawing stage allows you to plan, study and deconstruct the process you want to learn. The second stage is where you record your efforts at mimicking the process, where you record your failures and successes. It is this second stage that allows you to use drawing for learning, because you are externally projecting and visualising your inner struggle. I would argue that both processes are equally valid.

I hope I've convinced you that drawing in four dimensions is a really valuable learning tool, but it is only when you actually try it that you see its potential for learning.

The format for this kind of drawing is really important. We live in an A4, A3 metric paper sized world, but I have found that long paper rolls are more suited to this task, because they lend themselves (as cinematic film does) to record long series of sequential events. With A4 paper it is harder to set things out sequentially. In all events however, it may be that a digital pdf scan is more useful.

What is important now is that you think how you might apply this technique. It would work really well to study actions that happen over time, such as literary texts, films, plays, geological events, scientific experiments, learning new skills or historical events.

It doesn't matter how 'good' the drawings are, or that some are more artistic than others. You don't need to colour them or render elaborate decoration either. In this process, there is a golden moment when the drawing has achieved its purpose; understanding has been reached. Any decorative, artistic actions past this point are superfluous. They might make the drawings clearer to an audience, they might win you an art prize, but the intent of this is not purely aesthetic.

Drawing in four-dimensions 1: Design and Technology

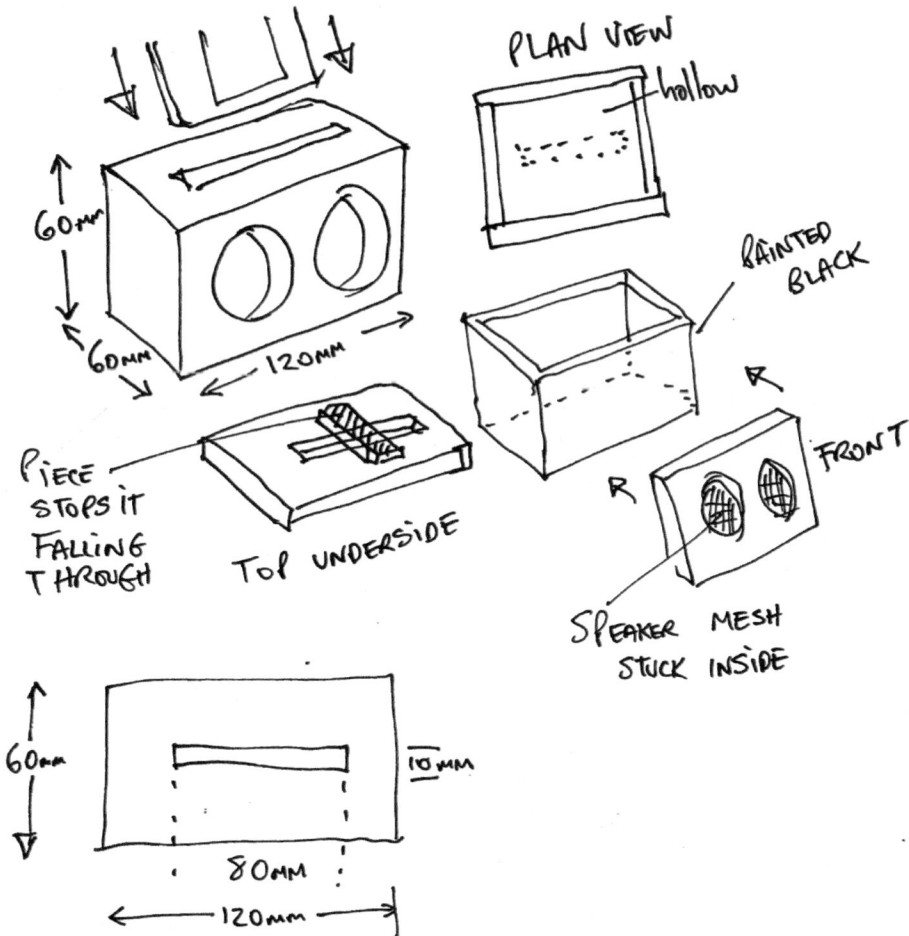

This is my design for a smartphone speaker holder. I've planned out the dimensions and figured out how I'm going to make it.

NEED:
5MM MDF, SPEAKER MESH, BLACK PAINT

STEP 1: CUT OUT PIECES

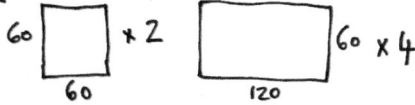

60 ☐ x 2
   60

☐ 60 x 4
   120

STEP 2: CUT OUT SLOT

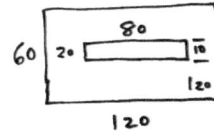

60 | 20 [80] 10 |
        120

slot wasn't wide enough for case

STEP 3 CUT OUT FRONT CIRCLES

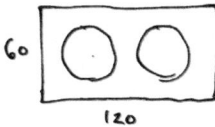

60 | ( ) ( ) |
      120

'Cut these badly, they weren't even.'

STEP 4: GLUE SPEAKER MESH

PVA

Kept falling off with the glue, needed staples.

STEP 5: FIX SUPPORT PIECES TO TOP

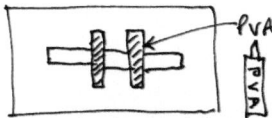

PVA

PVA

The slot should have been angled, so phone lent back

STEP 6: FIT TOGETHER

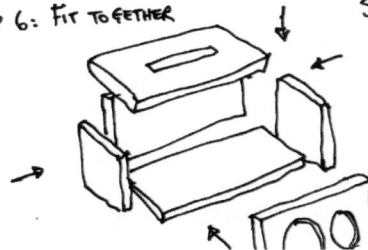

STEP 7: PAINT

PAINT

used wrong paint.

Then I drew a step-by-step instructional guide to making my box. This forces me to consider each stage and try to visualise what problems I will encounter. Notice also, the additional evaluation notes added AFTER I had made it.

Drawing in four-dimensions 2: Volcano formation

You could answer these questions using the process I have outlined:

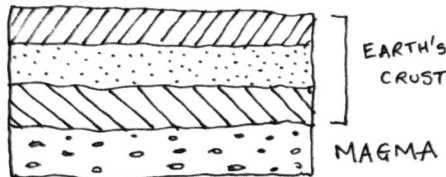

EARTH'S CRUST

MAGMA

1. What is magma and how is it formed?
2. Why does magma rise to the surface?
3. Use drawings to explain how:
   - Iclandic
   - Hawaian
   - Vulcanian
   - Vesuvian
   - Strombolian
   - Pelean

Eruptions occur.

Drawing in four-dimensions 3: Biology

Here I've laid out stages of fertilisation in a sequence to be read left to right. I added notes as an overlay on tracing paper. You could draw any biological sequence, then add overlays to explain what was happening.

6. DRAWING FOR MATHEMATICS

Drawing maths

Mathematics is a highly visual subject. The first archaeological evidence for mathematics comes in the form of tally marks and inscribings on cave walls, followed by small clay tablets dating from the Middle East over four thousand years ago. Always in maths we are using symbols, diagrams and marks to make internal thoughts external, so they can be understood by ourselves and others. Numbers are symbols themselves, but maths has added a whole plethora of other symbols to represent operations, instructions and formulas.

Number was considered by the Ancient Greeks and Pythagoreans to be the means by which the human mind could become closest to the Divine Mind. Interestingly though, they did not use numbers as we know them today, but rather pebbles or Khalix, which when translated into Latin becomes calcis and eventually became the word calculation we use today.

Stringing Khalix together became the abacus that many children still learn maths on. One pebble represented a point in space, two pebbles a line, three a triangular plane and four the square plane which developed into the first solid three-dimensional shape, a tetrahedron. I can visualise Ancient Greeks arguing over pebbles and lines strewn on the earth, as they formed the basis of what we now call mathematics. And this is a really important point; maths has always been visual, it has always been represented through objects and drawing, and that is why drawing is still so important to it.

Most mathematical textbooks, especially those in the primary phase, illustrate problems using visuals and diagrams. Visualising our inner mental thoughts and ideas is an important mathematical tool. We may or may not be visual thinkers, but all mathematicians need visuals in the form of diagrams, charts and graphs as a minimum.

It surprises many non-artists to learn that artistic drawing is a very mathematical pursuit. Constructing forms on a two-dimensional surface requires all kinds of mathematics: angles, lines, two-dimensional and three-dimensional shapes, geometry, measuring, proportion, size, ratio, scale and symmetry. Drawing is positively teeming with maths.

Humans usually aspire to create things with accurate geometric forms, constructed with neat edges, straight lines and precise angles. Nature isn't so precise. Its shapes and lines are irregular and organic. In maths rooms, you are taught that shapes are perfect circles, squares and triangles, but these shapes rarely exist in nature.

Drawing therefore, more closely aligns with the natural world, and you experience this when you draw human-made and natural objects, because organic forms are more forgiving. You don't need to be so precise, so they are easier to draw.

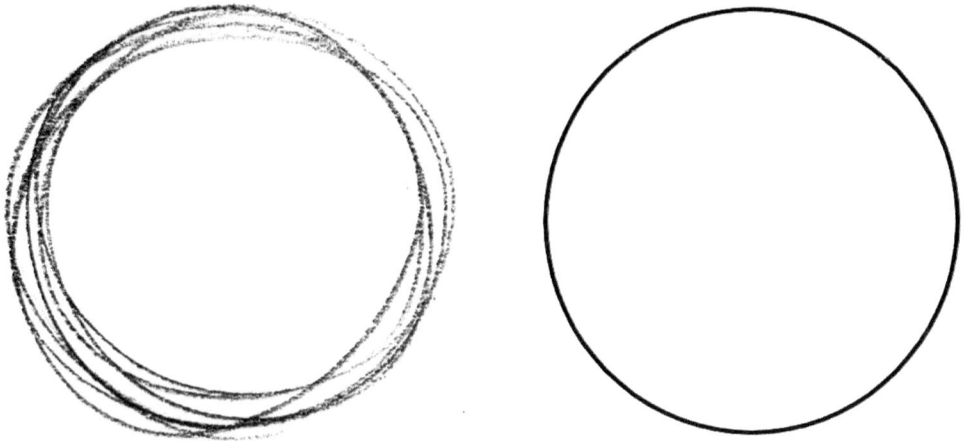

Two circles, one drawn with a computer is a 'perfect' shape,
the other drawn freehand is imperfect.

Playing with polygons

In basic geometry, a polygon is a plane figure described by a number of straight lines that connect to form a closed shape. Each line segment is called an edge or side, and the point where two edges meet is called a corner or a vertex. The inside of a polygon is called its body.

Most of the exercises over the next few pages will show you how to draw polygons within circles (cyclic polygons). This is a very simple exercise, so why does it matter? It matters because so much geometric mathematics is built on these simple foundations, which are often ignored.

You might learn that all the external angles of a regular polygon add up to 360 degrees, but if you know they do that because they are all based on a circle you can understand them better. Drawing polygons in circles was how the Greeks constructed early trigonometry, and this is important because it helps us to work out angles when we know the sides of triangles, and the sides of triangles when we know the angles. Trigonometry has been one of the major foundations of civilisation, from navigation to astronomy, to map making and construction.

Understanding the properties and relationships of polygons, in both the constructed and the natural world, is important to both the artist and the mathematician. There are simple polygons like the ones I'm describing here, but also complex ones, self-intersecting, abstract, spherical, star, skewed and apeirogon polygons, all with their own unique properties. Drawing them will help us understand them.

The first drawing is an equilateral triangle. Draw a point at 12 o'clock. Then another at 4 o'clock and another at 7 o'clock.

I have drawn polygons in a simple clock pattern. Circles where all the vertices (corners) of a polygon touch it are called circumscribed circles. Polygons of this type are called cyclic polygons.

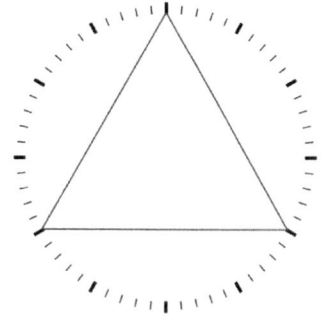

For a square, draw points at 12 o'clock, 3 o'clock, 6 o'clock and 9 o'clock and join them up. A five-sided polygon can be drawn by points at 12 o'clock, 11 mins, 23 mins, 37 mins and 49 mins.

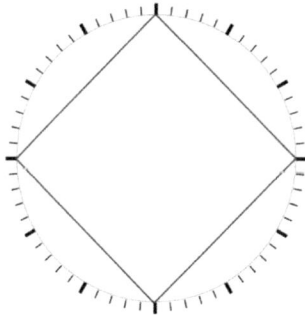

A 6-sided shape has points at 12, 2, 4, 6, 8 and 10 o'clock, An 8-sided shape has points at 12 o'clock, 7.5 mins, 3 o'clock, 22.5 mins, 6 o'clock, 37.5 mins, 9 o'clock and 52.5 mins.

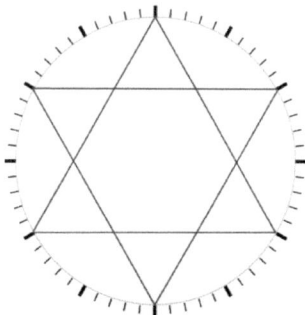

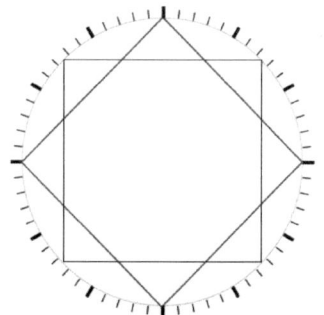

There is a big temptation when drawing for maths to use a ruler or other mechanical aids all the time, but I want you to resist your urges, because they slow you down and make you dependent upon them. They also fool you into thinking that you can't draw mathematically without them.

What I want to do now is to learn about polygons, so I've done some research and produced a sketchbook page of diagrams to teach me some basic principles. Your teacher usually teaches you this stuff, or you get it from textbooks. I've basically just copied some facts about polygons. I've copied some simple formulae for calculating angles and areas, but I'm not too interested in those yet, because I want to learn what polygons are and how they behave.

After I have completed my page of polygon studies, and learned what they are, I begin drawing them again mindlessly. I haven't got an aim in mind, I'm just drawing them repeatedly, building on drawings I find interesting and rejecting ones I don't.

Once you have some basic knowledge of polygons, you can begin to play with what you know and see where it leads you. I made quite a few pages of drawings of polygons.

I was more interested in irregular ones, and so I drew some out then traced them, trying to find if they made patterns or tessellated. My mind became full of questions such as does the formula for the angles of a regular polygon work with an irregular one. I decided it couldn't, but that the total of all the angles must still be the same.

Irregular polygons unequal angles + unequal sides

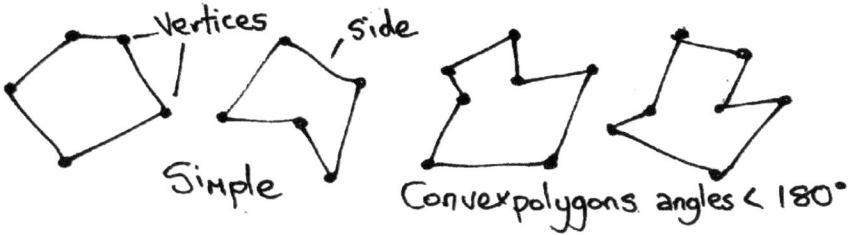

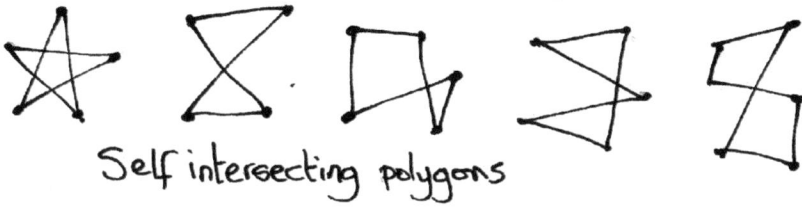

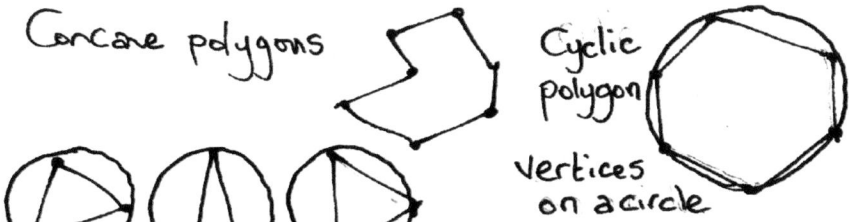

Vertices   side

Simple   Convex polygons angles < 180°

Self intersecting polygons

Concave polygons   Cyclic polygon

Vertices on a circle

Every triangle is cyclic

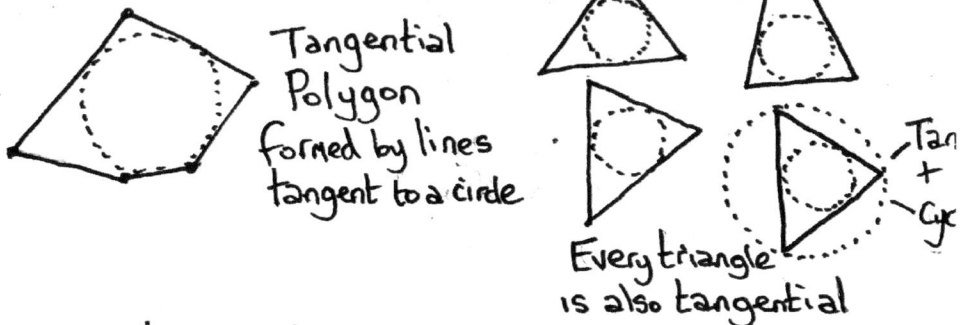

Tangential Polygon formed by lines tangent to a circle

Every triangle is also tangential

Tan + Cyc

n-gon interior angles
$$S = (n-2) \times 180° \text{ or } S = (n-2) \times \pi \text{ rad}$$
Sum Exterior angles = 360°

I am drawing freehand and learning at the same time.

I drew in pencil first, then went over it in pen.

I was especially interested in my cyclic polygons, so I began drawing them. I wanted to know how my star polygons would change in shape if I moved the points randomly, and I found that they always made irregular versions of it. This led me to an experiment of drawing six points on a circle, joining them into a set shape, then playing with moving the dots and changing the size of the circle.

My prior knowledge of biology made me realise I was actually rediscovering transformations of body shape, first proposed by Darcy Wentworth Thompson in his book On Growth and Form in 1917. He used a grid, but I found that circles will suffice. Mine were two-dimensional, but I'd like to experiment with three-dimensional, cell-shaped structures.

Now it may be that I am a brilliant genius, on a par with Darcy, but I highly doubt it because I know I'm not. The only explanation therefore must be that it is curiosity, experimentation and play that leads us to find new stuff out.

Curiosity keeps us wanting to learn long after the bell has gone. You need the hard, technical knowledge, but curiosity and playfulness can lead us to the maths and vice versa.

A note to teachers here: doing this with a class full of young, novice students might be problematic, but you could add focus to the task by asking questions and posing problems. The difficulty with this type of exploration is that it is like a hundred sheep running around a field. You need to harness the flow of the sheep, but not so much that they are terrified to move. This means being comfortable with uncertainty in your students, watch them scratch their heads in confusion, then germinate ideas around the group.

An interesting mathematical activity might be to plot a number of lines on a circle to create a form, then experiment with moving the points and altering the circle to create variations on the form. How might this work in a three-dimensional space?

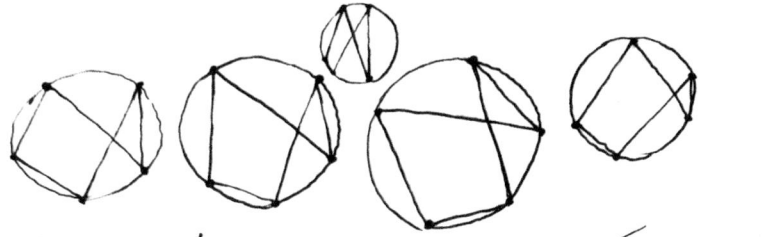

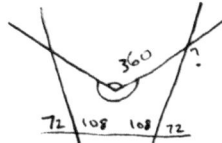

Concave pentagon

External angles = $\dfrac{360}{5}$

$72 \times 2 = \dfrac{360}{144}$
216

Would have to measure angles.

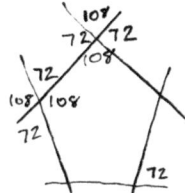

108×5
$= 540$
Sum of Int. angles

Regular

Irregular Shape
Formula Cannot Work
?
Irregular

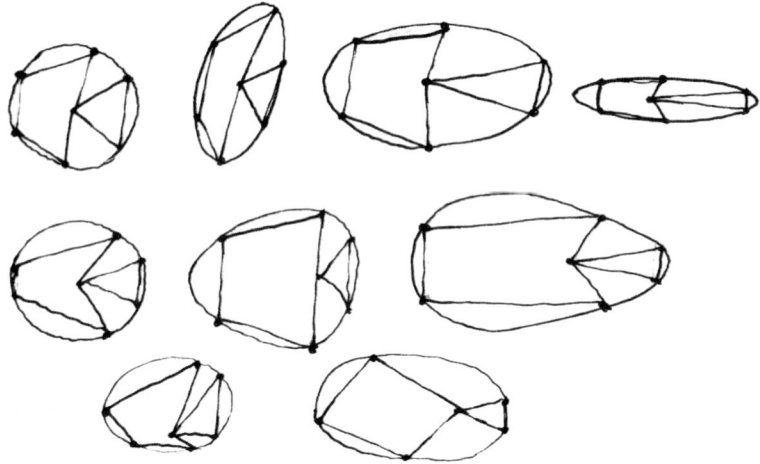

But that was not the end of my playing with polygons. Next, I decided to see how they behaved in three-dimensions, because I'm an artist and I think spatially. This is another string to the bow of drawing, because drawing so many three-dimensional forms on a flat surface enables me to think mathematically about forms (it's a shame I don't know the hard maths as well, because I could be actually good at it). My sketches led me to trying to draw polygons in three dimensions, and I worked out that I could use projections guidelines as they do in technical drawing to mark and plot the co-ordinates. Every mathematician in the country is begging me to use 3D axis here, which I thought about later, but the point is that I've got here by myself.

I have since learned how to do this exercise more accurately with 3D axis and there is some computer software that could do it better than me, but the point is that I have reached this point on my own, through curiosity and play. I can now easily transform any flat polygon into a three-dimensional form using drawing.

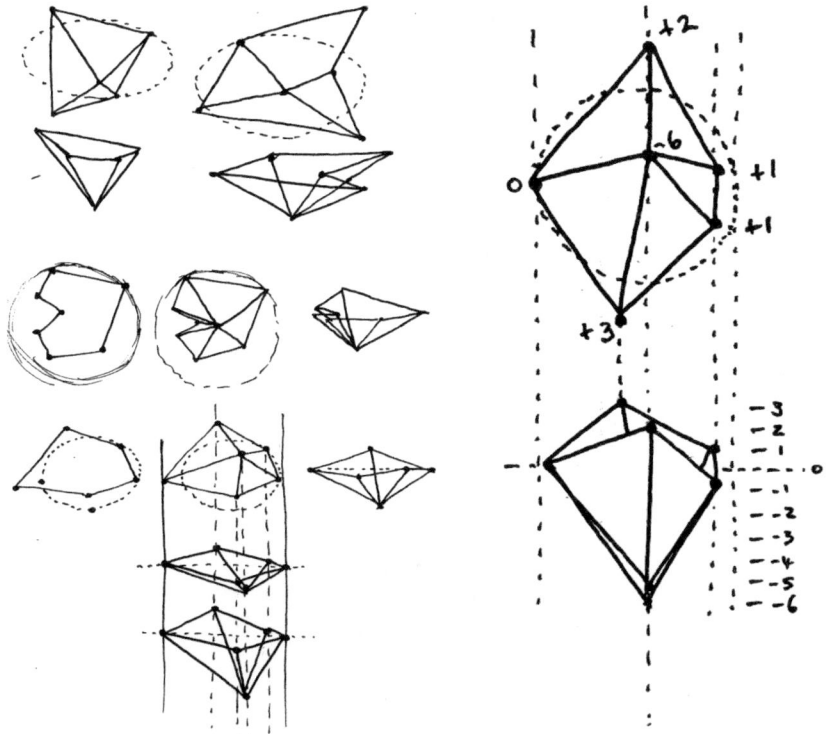

My explorations into polygons have been built on fragmented foundations of prior mathematical knowledge about shapes, research, my artistic skill and my interest in the subject. This may be hard for a teacher to replicate in a classroom, but you won't know until you try. You might begin with a demonstration of drawing a number of points on a circle randomly, then challenge students to draw as many variations as they can. My drawings joined to form a fish shape, but it could easily be a different creature. When they are exhausted of options, you might study Darcy Thompson's splendid transformation grids.

We need to incorporate maths lessons like this into our programmes of study. Drawing can and does lead us to all manner of intuition, discovery and happenstance. It doesn't matter how precise, accurate and neat the drawings are, only that they help us get our thoughts out onto a page.

Polygons are very interesting. They are everywhere, all around us and I have to say that they became much more interesting to me when I could draw them freehand, without rulers and precise angles. And their potential is enormous. Polygons are used to model and render characters, figures and backgrounds in computer games by means of a polygon mesh. This means that there is another property of them we can consider; that polygons can be joined to form continuous two- and three-dimensional forms. Computer game modelling gives us a whole new area to explore. I don't think my curiosity has abated yet but move on I must.

String patterns

We can create curves from straight lines and this technique was used for many years as an art form using string. The importance for the artist in doing this kind of drawing is to develop technical skill and precision; what is known as draughtsmanship. The importance for the mathematician is more profound. These simple patterns create parabolas and curves, themselves a fundamental part of studying efficiency and profit in business models using calculus, in physics for studying the motion of stars or space flight, for weather patterns, ocean currents, pollution, blood flow and for commercial building and product design. Bezier curves are used extensively in computer design, they help, not only to display and read information, but also to measure and predict it. We wouldn't have sent spaceships into space if we didn't understand curves, and a good place to start is with string patterns.

In maths, this curve is called a line envelope and the tangent lines themselves are called chords or segments. Curves of this nature are often parabolas. In computing they are known as Bezier curves and can be drawn from two fixed points.

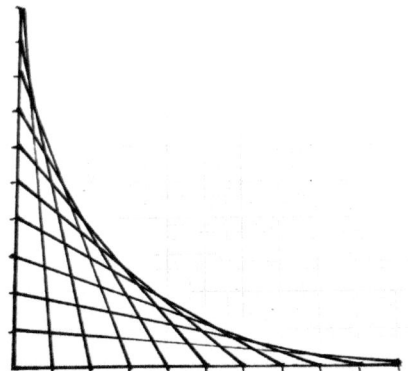

Let's begin with the easiest of string patterns, the right-angled curve. Draw a right angle on graph paper and begin by dividing each axis by ten. Draw straight lines from number one to number ten, two to nine, three to eight and so on until the pattern is complete. The resulting shape is not an actual curve, but a close approximation of one.

Once you have learned to do one of these patterns, you can join them together to make other patterns. It is a good idea to play with the spaces between the numbers, make them bigger or smaller, try to create different shapes and patterns. This playfulness is important to both artist and mathematician because it stretches the boundaries of what you know is possible. When you are familiar with drawing these with a ruler, try drawing them freehand.

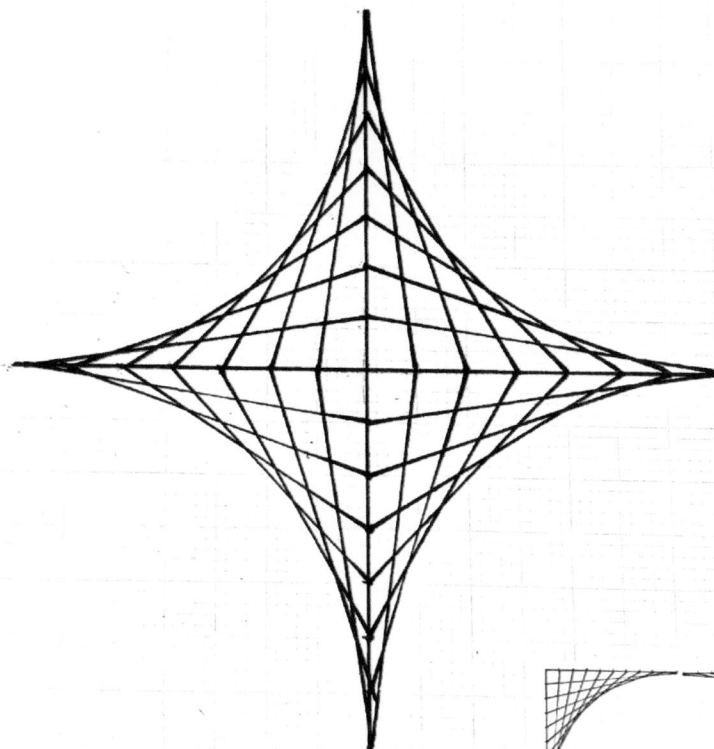

A four-sided string pattern that creates an interesting optical effect. Used one way and it creates a star shape, used another way it creates a circular shape.

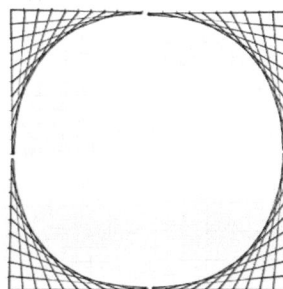

This circular string pattern is made by drawing a straight line from any point on the clock pattern to another ,and adding one-minute space after the beginning and end of the line. So it is the same line length travelling around the circle. The longer you make the first line the narrower the circle is in the middle. Go on to the internet and search string patterns to open up a whole world of geometry!

Circle patterns such as this are easy once you get the hang of them, though it is easy to make a mistake.

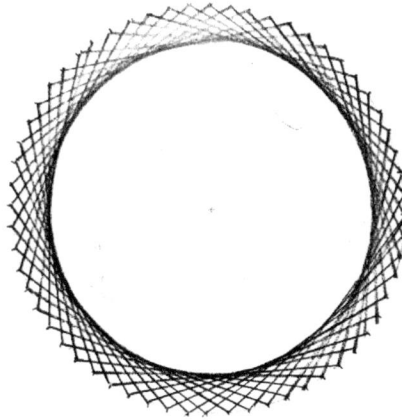

A cardioid pattern (heart shape) can be produced by drawing a line from 30 mins to 26, then 29 mins to 24, 28 mins to 22, 27 mins to 20, adding one unit at the beginning and two at the end each time. Then travel in the opposite direction from the 30 min mark.

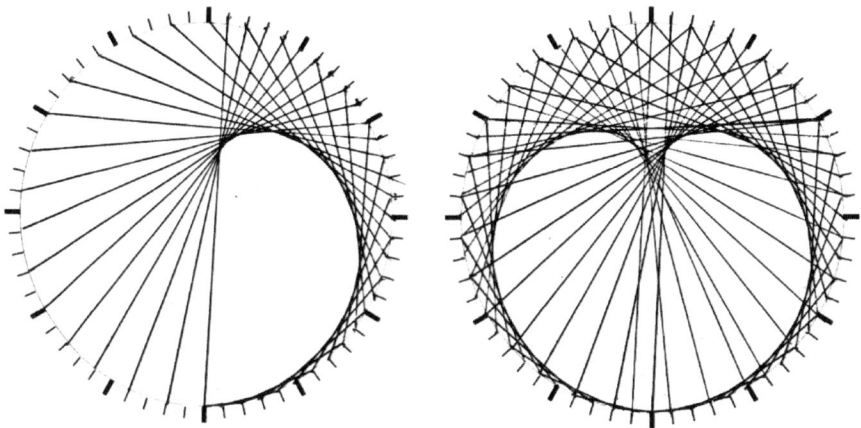

A true cardioid is a plane curve made by rolling a circle around another circle of the same size.

All of these string patterns are interesting mathematical operations, but so what? Is there any real point or purpose to learning them? They are at best a pleasurable pastime or a summer school maths activity to fill in time before students break up for summer, surely nothing more than that?

But now look at this engineer's design for a footbridge, produced by my brother Steve Carney at Origin Structures in Richmond.

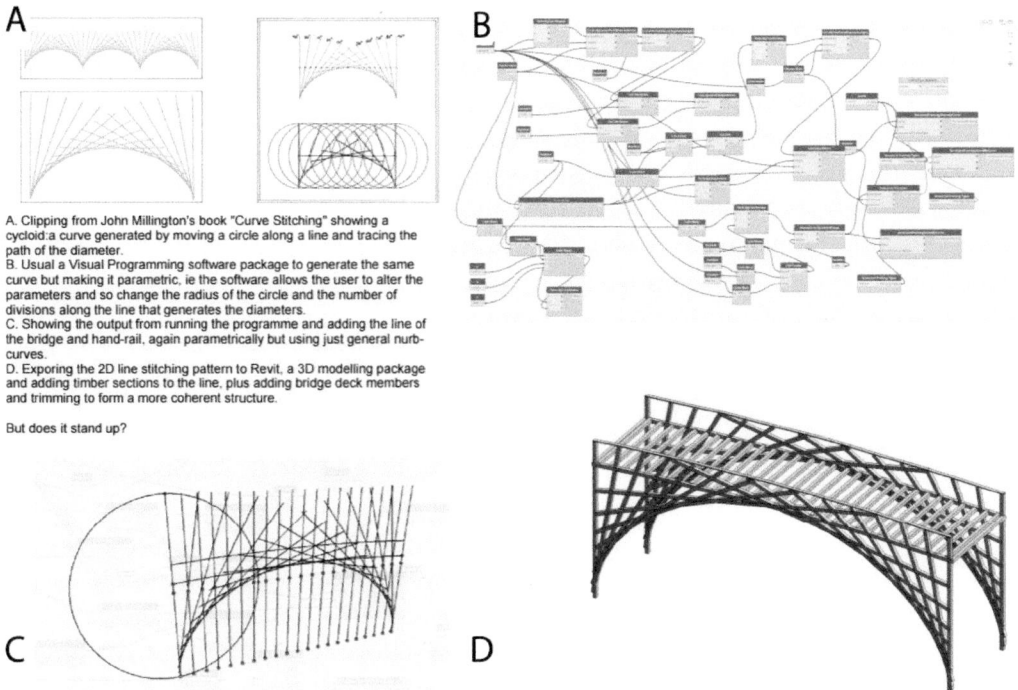

A. Clipping from John Millington's book "Curve Stitching" showing a cycloid: a curve generated by moving a circle along a line and tracing the path of the diameter.
B. Usual a Visual Programming software package to generate the same curve but making it parametric, ie the software allows the user to alter the parameters and so change the radius of the circle and the number of divisions along the line that generates the diameters.
C. Showing the output from running the programme and adding the line of the bridge and hand-rail, again parametrically but using just general nurb-curves.
D. Exporing the 2D line stitching pattern to Revit, a 3D modelling package and adding timber sections to the line, plus adding bridge deck members and trimming to form a more coherent structure.

But does it stand up?

Can you see how elegantly he has incorporated a simple string pattern into his bridge design? These mathematical principles may begin life as a simple childhood craft, but they go way beyond that and have potential for building, design and problem solving in the real world.

In a classroom situation, you might begin by drawing basic shapes with lines as I have shown you, but to really grasp it as a concept you have to apply it. I want to provide an example of a problem-solving situation where you might use or adapt string patterns in your learning.

Take this design scenario: *A County Council is proposing to build a bridge across a local river. They are looking for striking, original designs based around straight line patterns and they want you to come up with three design ideas. The designs must work practically and be as aesthetically pleasing as possible.*

We could set simple parameters to make this task easier, by stipulating this is to be a small footbridge 30 metres wide, and made from single-sized wooden beams. You might first try to make a model out of straws, string or cardboard and test it, before or after drawing it.

We could make it more complex by widening the river and stipulating that it is to be a suspension bridge 190 metres long. You might add cost restraints, ask for the practicalities of building it to be considered, or open the design parameters by adding Smart technology such as lighting the beams or traffic information points. You might set the load bearing values of the bridge and ask for calculations to be made of additional forces and tolerances. Suddenly our simple bridge design task using string patterns has become a very advanced challenge.

But at some point, whatever level you decide for this challenge you will come back to drawing. Now you can use a computer, a ruler and accurate measuring devices, but I would argue that if you can doodle it first, if you can visualise it, then you will begin to understand the meaning of gesture and how the form flows with the gesture.

This is really what good structures do. The form follows the flow of load force through the structure to the ground. So the form is a gesture to carry the loads. It can be seen in all types of structures, and it is how the great architect Frank Gehry creates his buildings. They begin as a gestural drawing on a piece of paper. This is where maths, engineering and art come together to create beautiful forms.

Design sketches for a suspension bridge using the string pattern technique. What is important at this stage is producing a flowing, eye catching design. Rulers and drawing aids would stifle the creative nature of the exercise. The mathematics, problem solving and engineering would come later.

Seeing geometry

I spent many years drawing and photographing flowers, obsessed by the mathematics hidden within them, and at times I wondered if this were the product of supernatural design by a higher being. Going back to the Greeks' Khalix you can see why this doesn't need to be the case. If I take a random number of pebbles, say five, and group them together as they may be arranged in a seed or a bud, I can replicate how they will grow by gradually moving them away from their germinating bud. If all five pebbles move at exactly the same rate, they'll form a perfect pentagon on a flat surface. But in nature, shapes aren't usually perfect. This is because in nature we are dealing with three dimensions, and in any case, some petals get more nutrition or sunlight and so grow more than their sisters who are positioned in the shade.

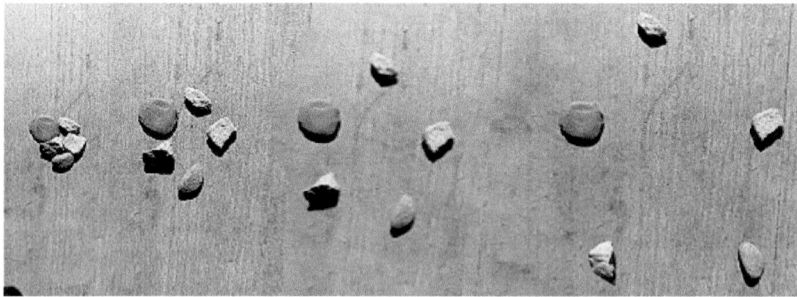

Geometry in nature is the product of the organism growing in the most efficient order, using the resources it has available. What we interpret as 'beauty' is the product of its own growth patterns.

Let's look at some basic shapes in nature and relate these to drawing. A flower when viewed from above is rich in geometry. If you study the flower closely you can identify irregular shapes (they are irregular even in this very good specimen). Two isosceles triangles overlap to create a hexagon. There is also a hexagon formed by the stamen and a triangle at the centre.

We can investigate the properties of the flower even further, to identify lines of symmetry and rotation, although again, these are approximate because these are irregular shapes. This is only the beginning of the flower's geometry, however. Not only could we identify many other shapes in this picture, but we can consider more lines of symmetry and rotation, we can look at angles and consider the similarities and differences between flowers of the same type and ask ourselves why this is.

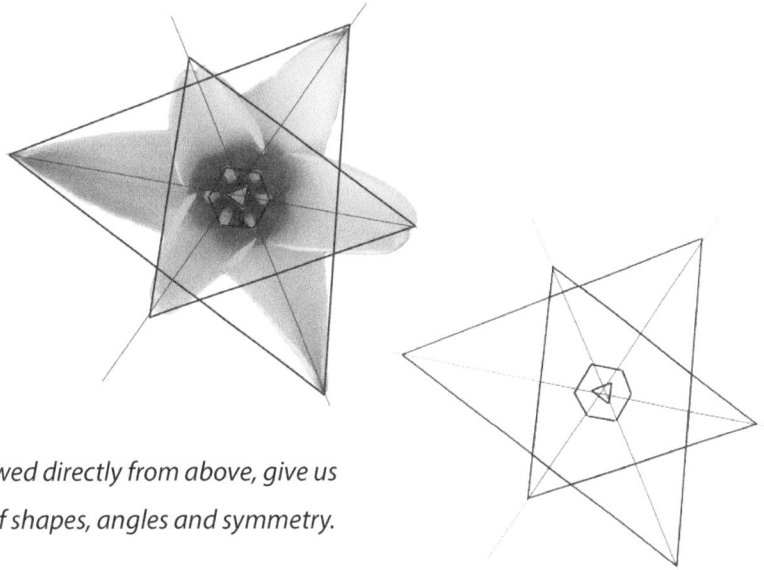

*Flowers, when viewed directly from above, give us
a fantastic array of shapes, angles and symmetry.*

Flower geometry

Flowers have an incredible geometry to them, and my diagrams only begin to touch the surface of the mathematical world they contain, but I want to show you why this geometry is important to the artist. Let me show you some of the stages I went through to draw an iris.

Armed with my knowledge of geometry I draw a centre point, followed by three axes. Then I measure points along each axis to correspond to the sizes of each petal.

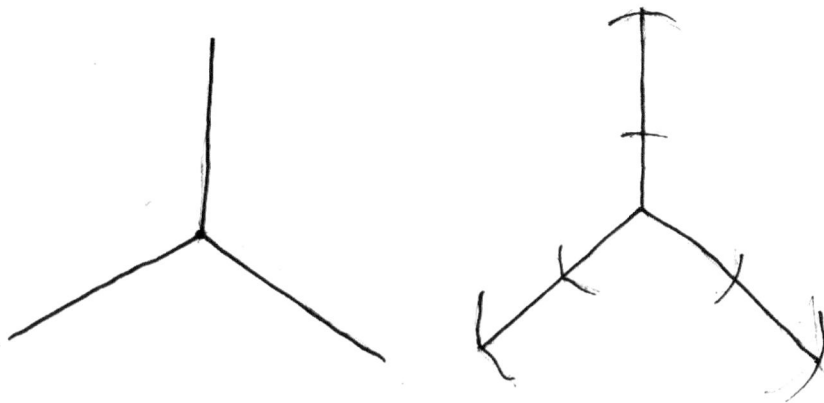

Once I've measured the iris and have the correct proportions, drawing it is much easier.

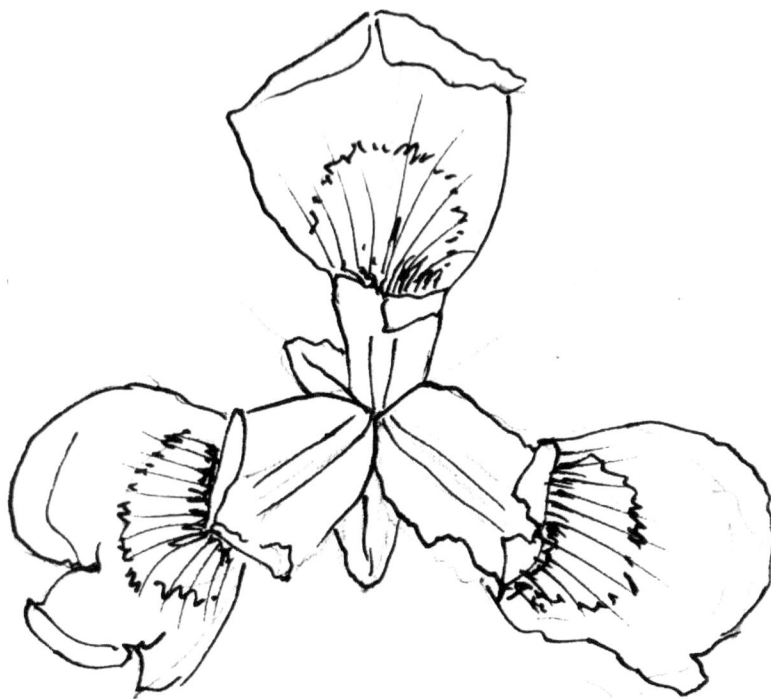

Drawing flowers freehand, without rulers teaches us a basic understanding of geometric form we can apply in our maths lessons.

Okay, now it's your turn. Find some flowers and take photographs of them directly from above. Examine the geometry in them. Compare flowers of the same species from the same plant. Can you see their similarities and differences?

We can draw the shapes we see in flowers (and other forms) by breaking them down into more formal shapes. Whilst not specifically regular shapes, it is very useful to both the artist and the mathematician to understand the underlying structure behind what they see, then draw it. For example:

I've traced some flower photographs (please don't be put off by my drawings) then sketched them mathematically. I can understand the symmetry of the flower, its angles, rotations, divisions, vertices and edges. As an artist, I'd use these mathematical divisions to help me measure and draw the flower.

Next, I have tried to reconstruct the flower petals using more formal shapes. You might even provide regular shapes and see if you can reconstruct the flower using them. This might lead you into exercises in calculating perimeter, area or even angles.

The complex shapes found in petals and leaves can be reconstructed using regular shapes. When we know and understand this it helps our drawing ability, but we can also use this knowledge to inform our mathematical understanding of shape and form.

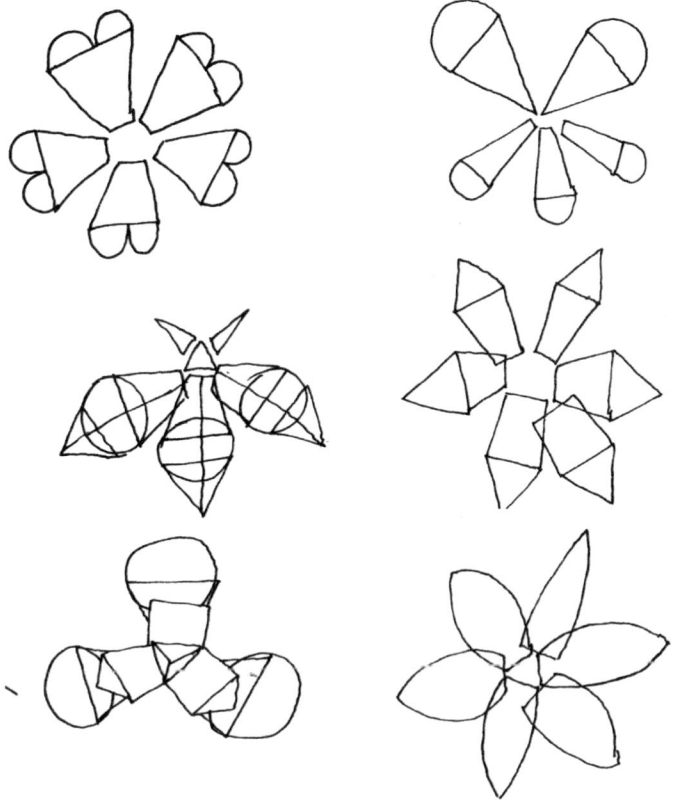

It is not just flowers that display such amazing geometry. Look at all manner of natural forms, seed pods, leaves, even viruses have such a beautiful organisation to them, thanks to the evolutionary power of efficiency. It is a profound learning exercise to try to unravel the basic geometry of all kinds of life forms.

German biologist and naturalist Ernst Haeckel made some of the most beautiful studies in this field and it is always worth studying his gorgeous illustrations, most of which are available online. Being able to recognise and identify the many different mathematical aspects of the world around you is important. If I know how to identify the basic underlying shape from which the object is constructed, I can draw it better. So the maths leads us to the drawing and the drawing leads us to the maths.

Here the student has sketched the geometric proportions of the flower first to guide her into making a more accurate drawing.

Compass geometry

I am old enough to remember using a compass in maths lessons to draw arcs and to plot points and angles, but I don't believe they are used very much, if at all in maths lessons these days. It's a shame because they are quite brilliant for drawing and far more rewarding than drawing them on a computer. I'm going to show you how to do the flower of creation using a compass. You may think that starting to draw compass flowers with a six-sided hexagon would be a hard place to begin, but in fact, it is easier than many of the other shapes.

How to draw the Flower of Life

First you need draw a circle with a compass. Keep the compass the same width at all times.

Then, set the compass point at the twelve o'clock position (approximately). Then draw an arc from edge to edge.

Place the pencil point at the place where the arc crossed the circle and place the compass point on the circle. Be as precise as you can. Draw another arc. Repeat this last step until all arcs have been drawn.

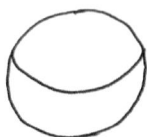

You can create a never-ending pattern by drawing full circles instead of arcs and overlapping them.

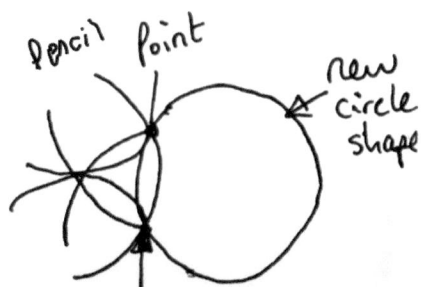

How to draw an equilateral triangle

Draw a vertical line between points A and B.

Set your compass to the mid-point of line AB and draw a circle.

With your compass still fixed to the same setting, place its point at B and draw an arc through the centre to make points C and D where the arc touches the circle. Join points A, C and D to make a triangle.

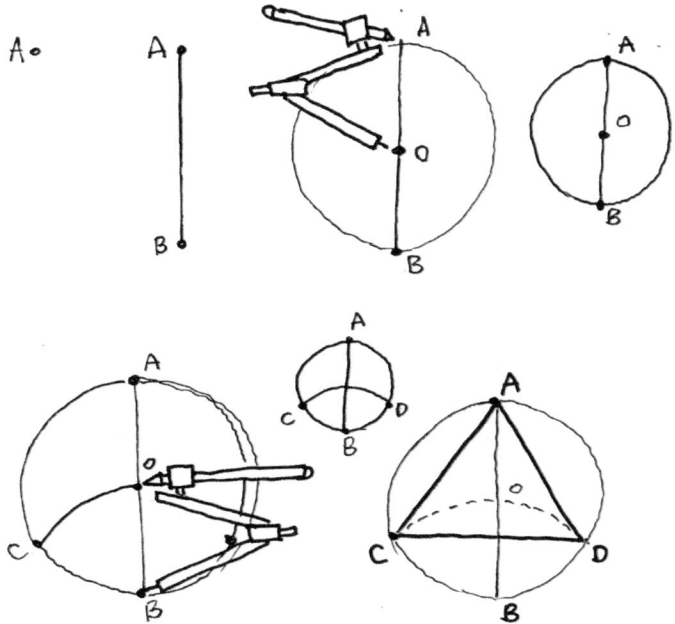

To draw using a compass, use a sharp pencil and make sure the compass is not loose. Practice drawing circles first to get the hang of it.

You can now create a three-sided flower, which in biology is called a monocot. Monocot flowers often have both a rotational symmetry of three and three mirror lines. A good challenge is to see if you can repeat the circles to form a continuous design.

How to draw a square

Draw a horizontal line between points A and B. Set the compass width to the length A, B. Use this setting to draw a circle with radius A, B and centre point A.

Now place the centre point at point B and draw another circle that passes through point A.

Using a set square, with horizontal at line AB, draw a vertical line from A to the top of the circle to make point D.

Repeat this line from point B upwards to make point C where the new vertical line meets the circle. Join points A, B, C and D to make a square.

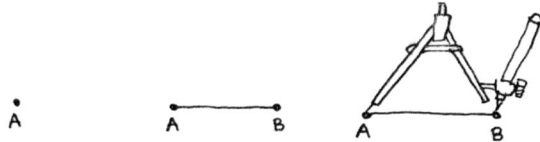

It is possible to draw the square using only the compass, but I find it a bit tricky. This method using a ruler and set square will work.

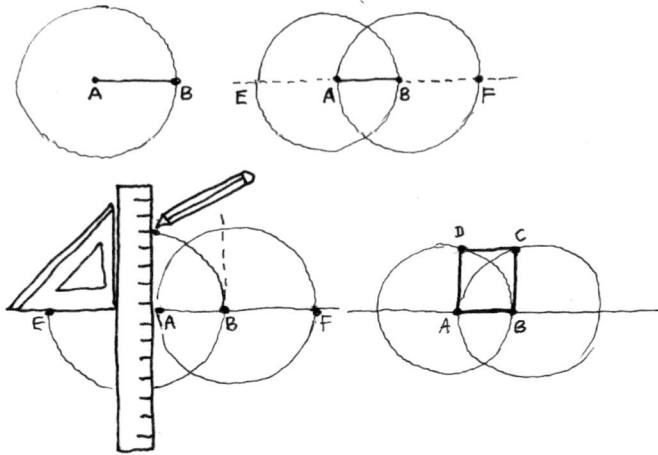

You can now create a four-circle pattern. A good challenge is to see if you can repeat the circles to form a continuous design.

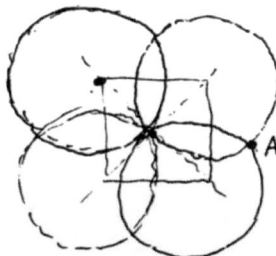

How to draw a pentagon

This is quite hard but give it a try!

Repeat the square diagram from the previous exercise.

Draw a central vertical line where both circle cross to make point O at the intersection between line AB.

Set compass to points OC. Draw a 180-degree arc to meet the horizontal AB and create points G and H on this line.

Set the compass at points AH and draw an arc to meet the vertical through O. This will create points J where it meets the circle and K where it meets the vertical.

Repeat this arc on the opposite side with the compass set at BG to create point L where the arc crosses the circle.

Join points ABJK and L.

The five-sided pentagon is the hardest shape to draw, even harder than six- or seven-sided shapes. Is there a mathematical reason for this?

Draw the square diagram shown previously

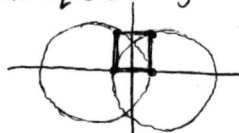

place compass at o, E

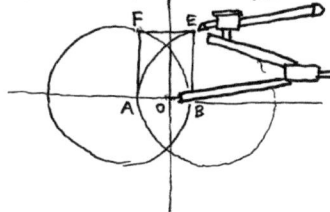

Draw an arc to meet horizontal at G, H.

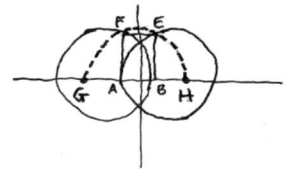

Put Compass at A, H then draw an arc to vertical

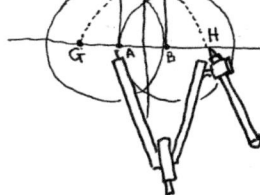

This will make J, K

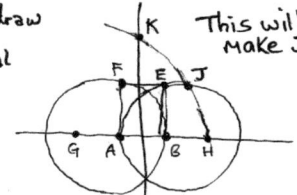

Repeat this on the other side from B and G to make an arc that cuts the vertical. This will create point L.

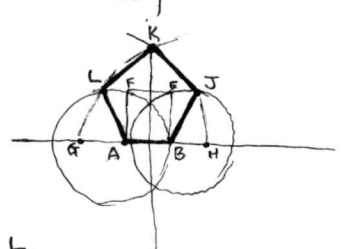

Creating more complex patterns from a compass

Look at this illustration to see one example of how the flower of life pattern I showed you earlier has been used by Islamic artists over centuries to create the most beautiful geometric patterns. The same flower of life pattern can be used in so many different ways to create a whole variety of patterns. This is where nature, maths and art merge to create stunning images. What I've shown you is a starting point into the world of art and maths, it is up to you if you want to explore it.

This Islamic pattern uses the Flower of Life hexagon geometry to create a beautiful mathematical pattern. There are many many more variations on this. Can you design some?

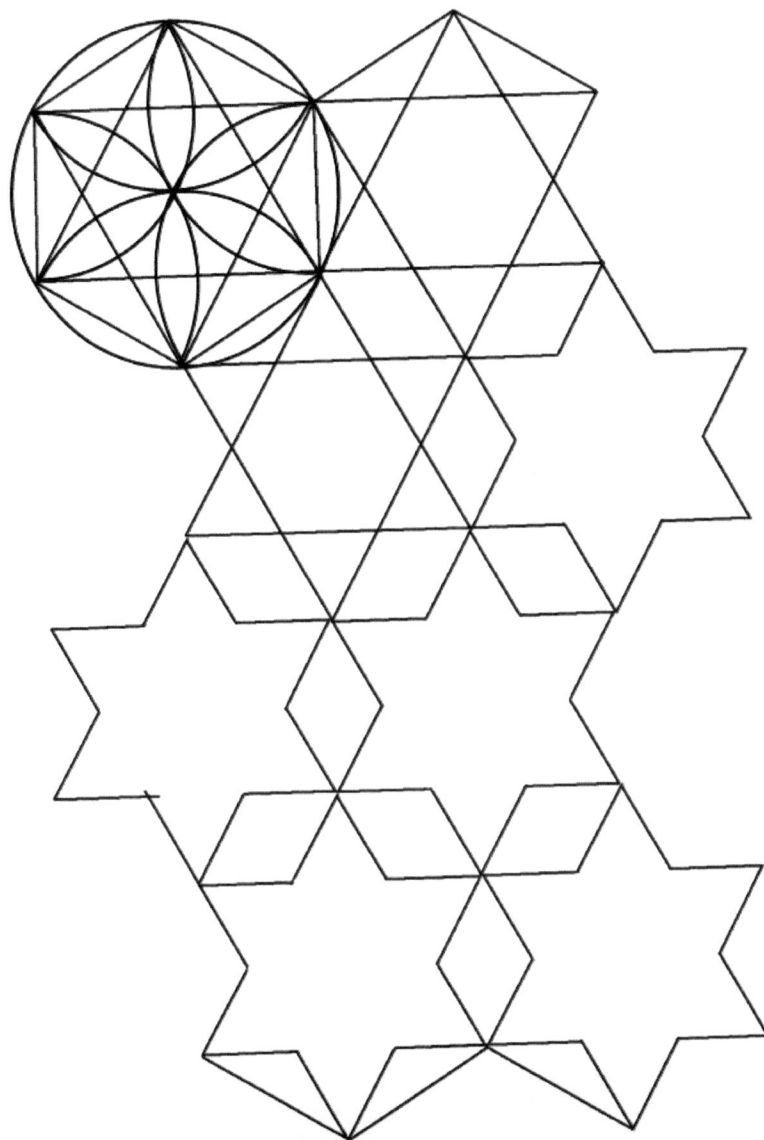

Drawing patterns

Drawing two-dimensional shapes leads us to another important area of maths and art, and that is pattern making. Patterns are everywhere. You find them in nature on animals, insects, birds, reptiles, fish and flowers. You see them on buildings and architecture, they are on our clothes, on our pottery, wallpaper and furnishings. They are artistic but also very mathematical. Essentially, any motif (a shape used to make a pattern) can be repeated to make a pattern.

But before we look at pattern making with motifs, we need to design a motif. We can use any shape we invent for this purpose, but ever since patterns were invented they have been heavily influenced by nature. So let's start there and draw some natural forms. If my drawing looks a little daunting for you, remember you can trace from pictures if it helps.

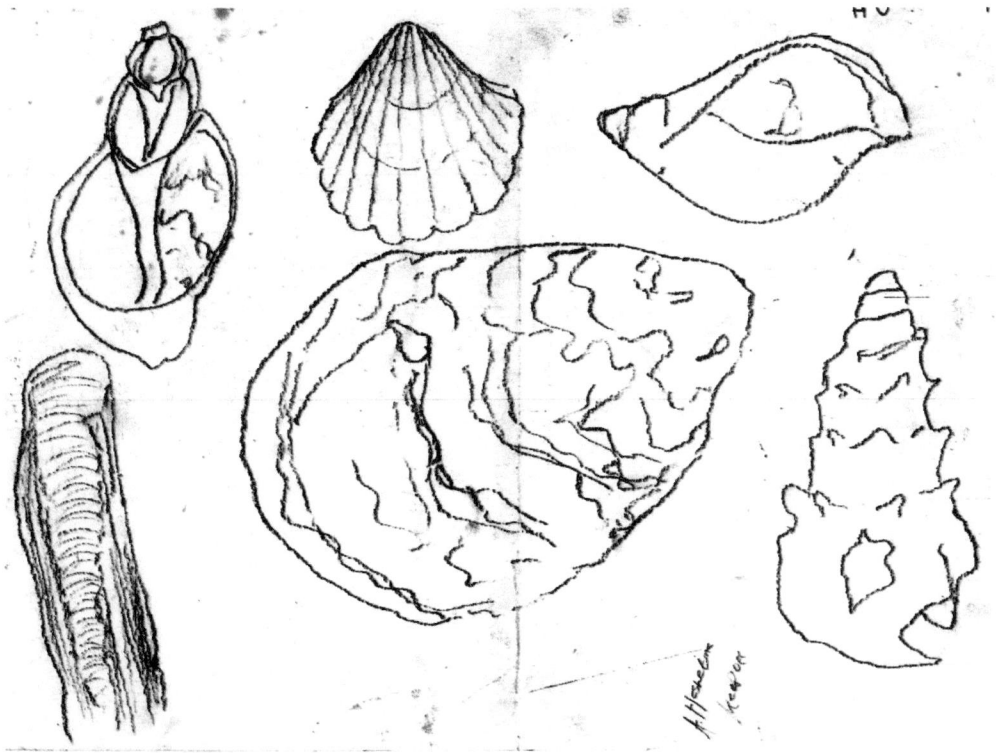

I've drawn some shells from observation because I loved their shape.

Next, you'll need tracing paper to trace your favourite motif and some squared paper, preferably large sheets of it if you can get it. Then trace your design on both sides of the tracing paper and begin setting them out on the squared paper into a design. In setting out your patterns you can think about flipping the motif, rotating it, overlapping it and maybe only selecting areas of it in places. What you should do is to use the squares to count and measure the spaces in between your designs. Here are some ideas I have done using my earlier drawings:

I set out my motifs in circular symmetry using both mirror and rotational images. It looks great, but I haven't spaced them out correctly. On the second design, I've again flipped and rotated my motifs, only now I've added some extra drawing of my own to fill the spaces.

Thinking about how your pattern will continue off the page is really important. This is called 'repeat pattern' and there are many elaborate ways of doing repeat patterns. Here is an example:

Some final designs for my fabric based on my shell drawings.

Draw a simple motif on to neoprene foam. Divide it into four pieces and number them.

Glue the pieces diagonally opposite each other on to card using PVA glue. Add a second motif in the centre.

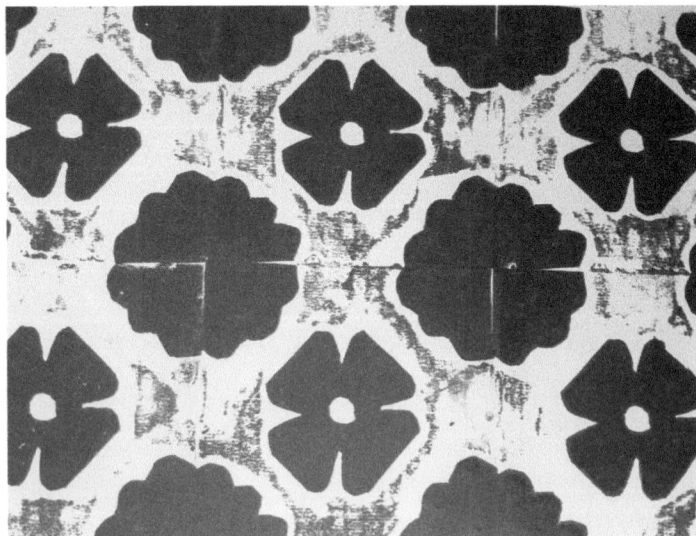

Then print the block side by side on to large paper.

Drawing growth patterns

Drawing can be very difficult at times, because sometimes what you're looking at seems too complicated to represent. Don't worry, information is often complicated and also, you might not have the patience to draw every blade of grass on a lawn you are drawing. It isn't just the amount of information that is hard to draw, it is often the way it is set out and this is beautifully demonstrated when drawing nature.

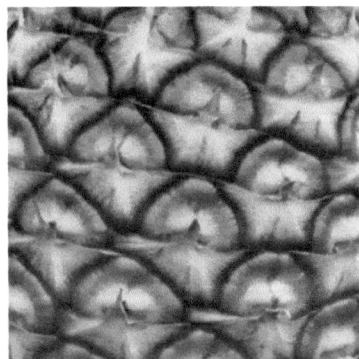

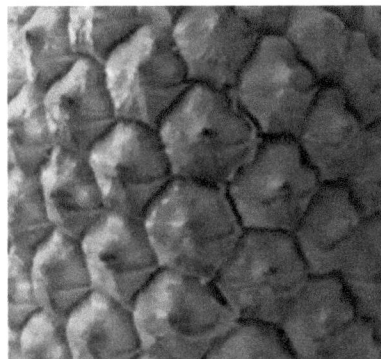

Pineapple photos.

Take this pineapple. Before you draw anything, you should look at it closely to try to understand it. When you look at pineapples, they have different growth patterns according to the type they are.

These patterns are interesting and quite different to draw. Let me show you. The pineapple on the left is easy enough. I can draw one set of parallel diagonal lines one way, then another equidistant set in the opposite direction.

I have to draw parallel lines slightly curved because the fruit is round. This is difficult to do at first, so trace them if it helps.

The second pineapple pattern is much harder to draw because the previous method doesn't work. Plants tend to grow in spirals, and they don't always produce a petal or pineapple chunk at every spiral because they would get in each other's way.

I have tried the same method to draw the second pattern but it hasn't worked.

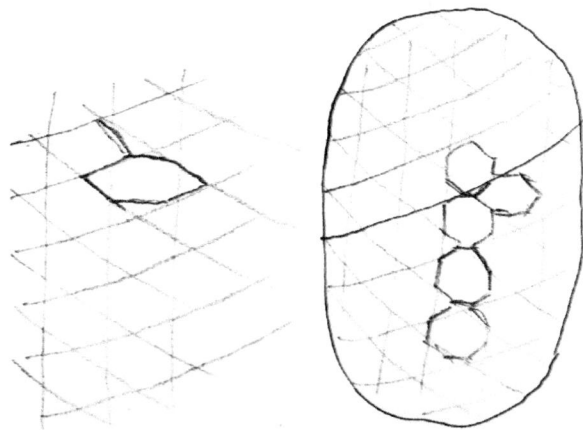

The first pineapple pattern has two sets of spirals that criss-cross, hence we can draw them easily with two sets of parallel lines. The second pineapple has three sets of spirals however, each spiral aligned through opposite sides of the hexagon shapes. This is why my first method did not work when drawing the second pineapple.

Pineapple drawing with three spirals.

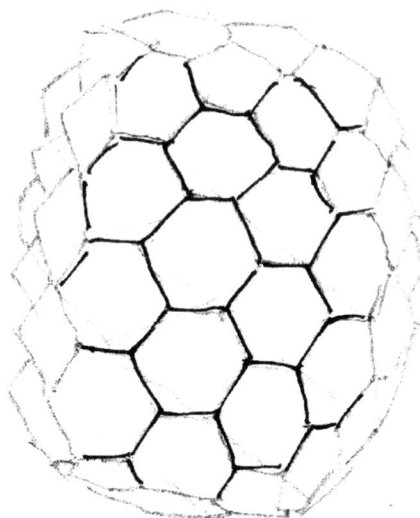

This type of growth pattern is called the Fibonacci sequence and you can see it on all kinds of plants, such as blackberries, beech, pine cones, palm trees, oaks and elms. The Fibonacci sequence states that each number in the sequence is the sum of the two numbers that precede it. So you begin with 1, then the next number in the sequence is 1 (because the number before it is a 1), then there is a 2 (1+1) then a 3 (1+2) then 5 (2+3) and it continues like this:

1, 1, 2, 3, 5, 8, 13, 21, 34, 55, 89…

A Fibonacci ratio is any Fibonacci number divided by another Fibonacci number so 5/8 for example or 5/13 or even 8/5. These sequences are all over the place: from the finger bones of your hand, to pinecones, music, art and even in space. So if you know the maths, you can understand the growth pattern and so draw it more easily.

Let's look at another example to show you how. Sunflowers grow in two sets of spirals, one going clockwise and the other anti-clockwise. If you count the number of spirals in each direction, they will nearly always be numbers from the Fibonacci sequence, usually 34 going one way and 55 going the other, according to variety.

Flower Fibonacci spiral photograph.

Drawing these spirals isn't easy and I would hardly ever draw the exact Fibonacci number, but it helps me to know it is there. When I understand the growth pattern, as an artist I can work out how to draw it. I always have to figure out how to draw complex things, I don't just make it up or it goes wrong and an understanding of maths is key to helping me. So I drew spirals in one direction and then some in the other direction, before adding the actual seed heads of the flower. Notice I haven't drawn the exact Fibonacci number of spirals. It depends on how exact I want my drawing to be.

Notice that each line of this Fibonacci spiral has a curve that changes as it rotates around the flower head. It is very difficult to draw this correctly and takes lots of practice.

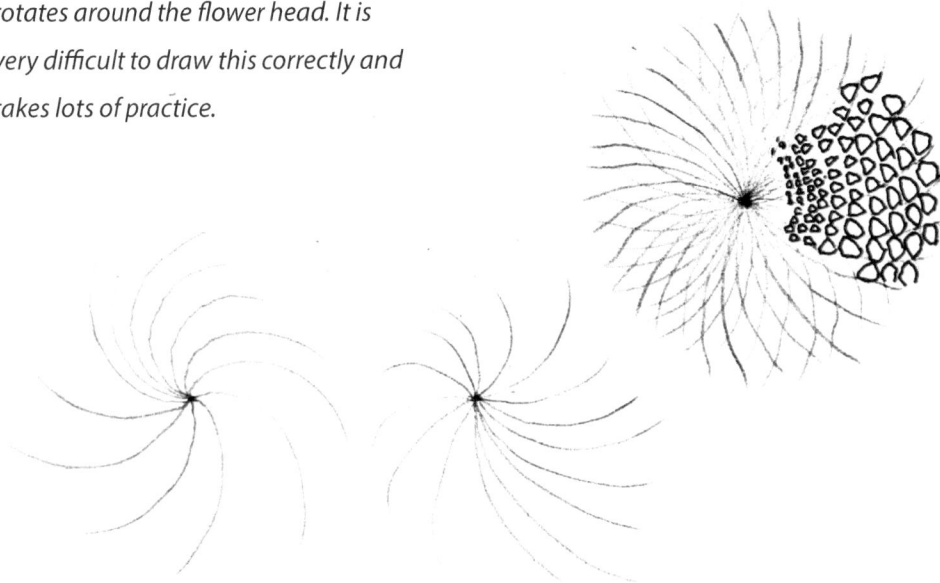

Drawing three-dimensional shapes

Being able to draw three-dimensional shapes freehand, without a ruler is one of the core skills of drawing. It is also a skill that can help students' mathematical ability in many ways, because doing it successfully depends on your ability to visualise three dimensions in your mind and this isn't easy. Visualisation of three-dimensional shapes begins with pre-school play, making towers from blocks, fitting shapes into holes and constructing shapes with straws.

You learn three-dimensional shapes in greater depth in Key Stage 1 and build on this knowledge repeatedly through your school life. They are important to mathematicians, engineers and architects as well as computing and games design among other fields such as physics and astronomy. If we can draw these shapes freehand without rulers, we will become both more confident artists and better at visualising shapes that will aid our maths.

One of the first tests I used to give my new art students was to draw a freehand cube. Even at age fourteen, many simply could not do it. In fact, many adults can't do it either.

Typical cube drawing results.

Here is how I used to teach my students to draw a cube. Write the letter Y shape, keeping the arms of the Y at about 45-degree angles. Draw mirror images of the Y arms at the bottom of the line. Now, using your powers of visualisation, measure two vertical side lines of the square. If you put these lines too close to the centre line or too wide, you'll make a cuboid not a cube. Now copy the Y arms again to create a diamond shape on top. Check that your lines are parallel to the Y arms.

It helps to draw a cube if you begin by drawing the letter Y.

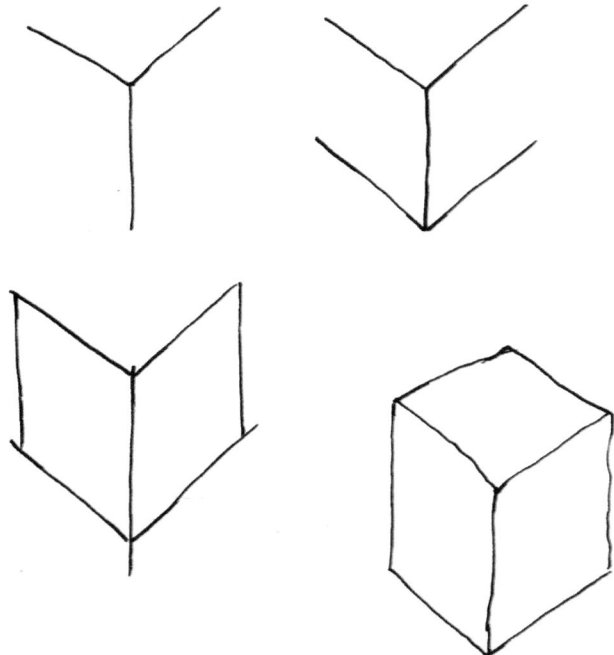

To draw a cylinder, draw two parallel lines. Then write the word OOOO in between them. Rub out the centre letters and you will have a cylinder.

Drawing the letter O within guidelines helps you see that you are drawing a solid 3D shape.

To draw a cone repeat the same process but begin by drawing the letter V on its side and make the letters O gradually bigger. Make sure you don't go over the lines. You will now have a cone.

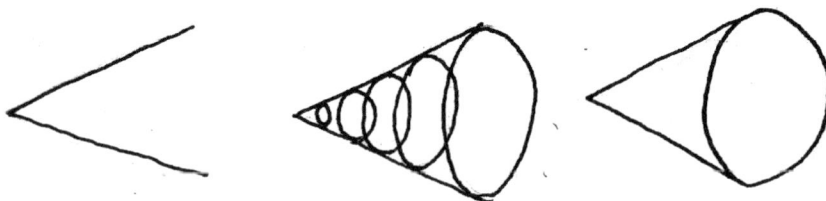

To draw a sphere is a little harder. I begin by drawing a square then divide it up into four equal sections. Draw diagonals in each box to make a rhombus. Now use the lines of the rhombus to create curved arcs for your sphere. Rub out all the guidelines and just keep the sphere shape. Draw the letter O again from top to bottom to create the curved shape.

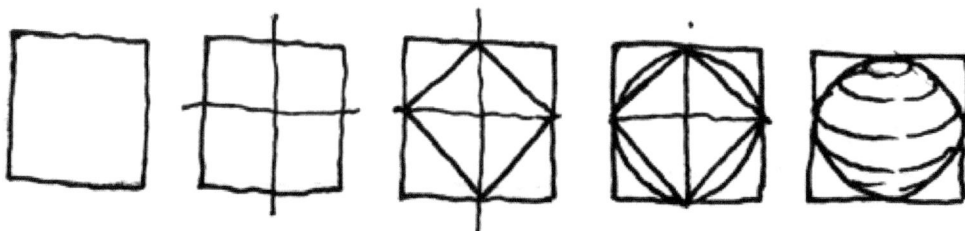

When you can draw three-dimensional shapes such as this freehand without a ruler, you will become a better artist. When you can adapt these shapes and make them different sizes you should be able to draw anything. Not only that but your ability to visualise mathematical problems that require visual spatial thinking will have improved too.

Being able to sketch out 3D shapes easily, then adapt them and manipulate them is key to drawing.

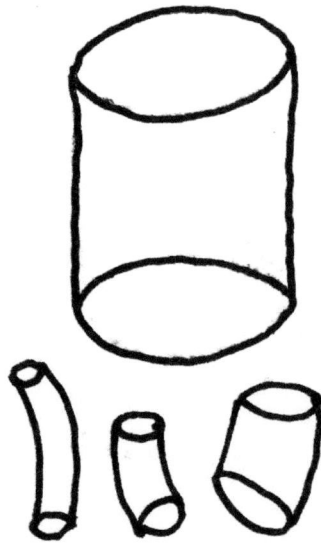

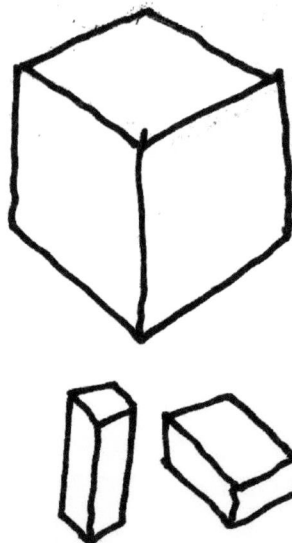

Once you can confidently draw 3D shapes from different angles you can move on to drawing packaging from observation. Once you've done that you might draw 3D letters or play with simple perspective. Drawing a cathedral is no different to drawing a cereal box. You draw cubes, then you mathematically divide them up to add detail and draw additional shapes.

If you recall the exercise early in the book I asked you to divide a straight line into equal proportions. You need this skill to draw the windows of the cathedral.

Drawing tessellations

In mathematics, a tessellation is the tiling of a surface using one or more geometric shapes, called tiles, with no overlaps and no gaps. They can be very simple, regular shapes such as squares, rectangles or triangles. You will be familiar with such tessellations because they are used to create bathroom or kitchen tiles.

Tessellations can be very complex, even artistic, as was demonstrated by the famous Dutch mathematician and artist MC Escher in the twentieth century. You can find examples of his stunning work very easily by searching for him in a browser and I guarantee you will be impressed. But before you see the really complex stuff, let's just get you drawing some simple freehand tessellations with a pencil and paper. No rulers, although you can use squared paper if it helps. Copy the examples if you need to.

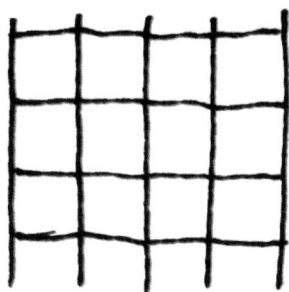

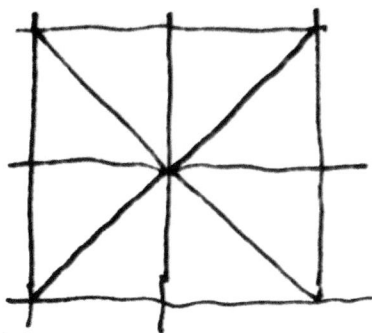

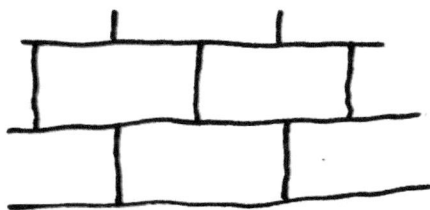

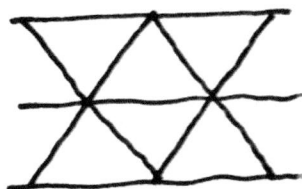

We can play with tessellations though to make them more interesting, because you can change their shape considerably as long as you follow a simple rule: what you take from one side you have to put on the opposite side.

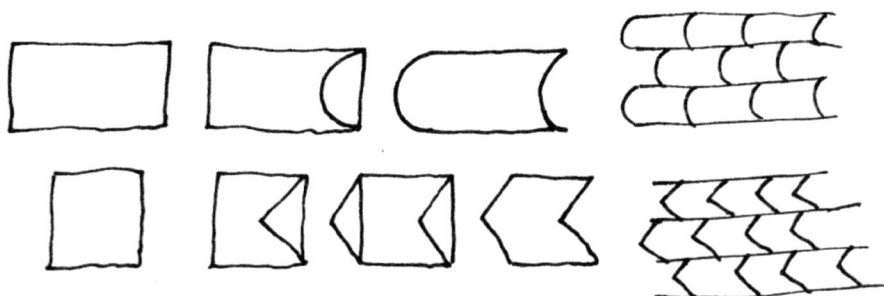

To create your own tessellations, remove a shape from one side of a regular shape and add it to the opposite side.

It's easy enough to alter regular shapes by adding and removing other regular shapes. Doing this creates some interesting patterns, but the point I'd like to make here is for you to try to do them freehand, without rulers because your drawing skills will improve. Not only that, but your maths skills will improve too, because you have to think spatially about which shapes will fit together. You are also improving important visualisation skills by learning how to flip, rotate and turn shapes.

This kind of geometric understanding of tessellations helps us to draw too. When you're drawing roof tiles, fish scales, pineapples, pine cones, bricks and architectural forms, for example, you are using your knowledge of mathematical shapes and forms. Maths isn't separate to drawing, it isn't a different skill, they aren't two completely different domains. Art and maths are two fields that overlap, and where they overlap is of interest to both artists and mathematicians.

Create your own tessellations by doodling on a piece of paper. Begin by copying ones you see, in nature or in books, then gradually add your own ideas and creations. Patterns are beautiful and fun to do.

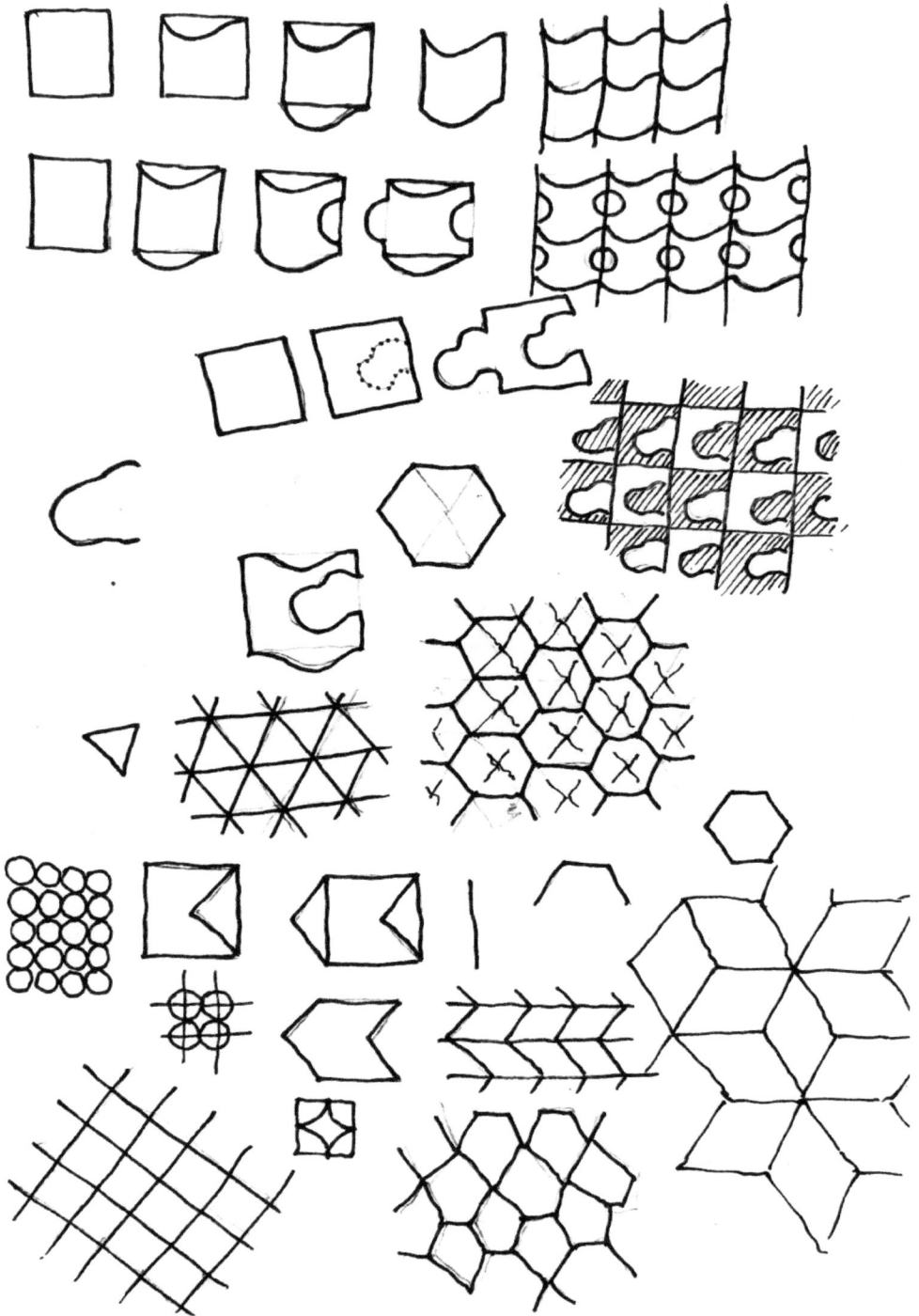

It's fun to just play with shapes and tessellations in a sketchbook. You'll improve your drawing skills and your mathematical ability at the same time.

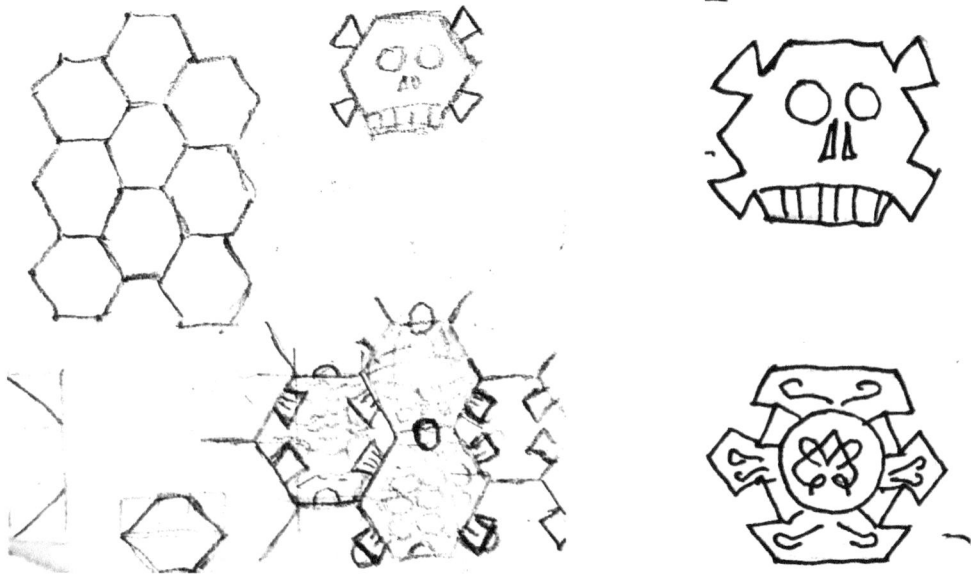

I took a simple hexagon tessellation and started playing with it using the rules I mentioned earlier— what I add on the outer edge I have to take out somewhere else. I played with the shape, trying to think of what it could become before I saw a skull design. This pattern uses two different hexagon tessellations—a skull and a Celtic cross. This needs drawing up more accurately now, but my design, my idea began in a simple sketch, tracing and copying patterns I liked.

148

Drawing for counting

Ever since consciousness evolved, people have made marks to represent numerical value. Tally marks exist throughout prehistory, so the act of making one mark to represent one thing is as old as human beings are. At the same time as having to learn our complex language system, children must also learn that a set of abstract symbols we call numbers represent numerical values.

This is challenging for many pupils, and one of the difficulties is learning that the symbol we draw for a number is equal to a set value of things. As we progress, we must learn how to group and multiply these symbolic values, and this can have profound implications for students who are already struggling to grasp basic symbolic value in numbers.

The most common method of relating number symbols with their value is the dot method. This method helps teach the value of numbers, but it does not associate them with the symbol for the number.

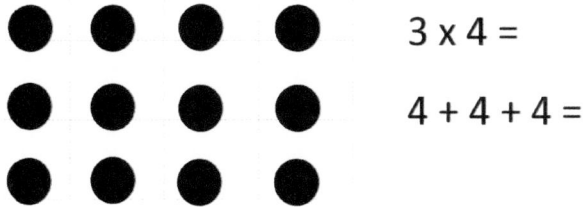

$3 \times 4 =$

$4 + 4 + 4 =$

One way I thought of that could overcome this, is by creating a number font that encourages pupils to draw tally marks within the number symbol.

There are no spaces to put tally marks in the nought, one space in the number one, two spaces in the number two etc.

0   **|**   **2**   **3**

Nought   **One**   **Two**   **Three**

This system should enable children to match the number system with its value more easily.

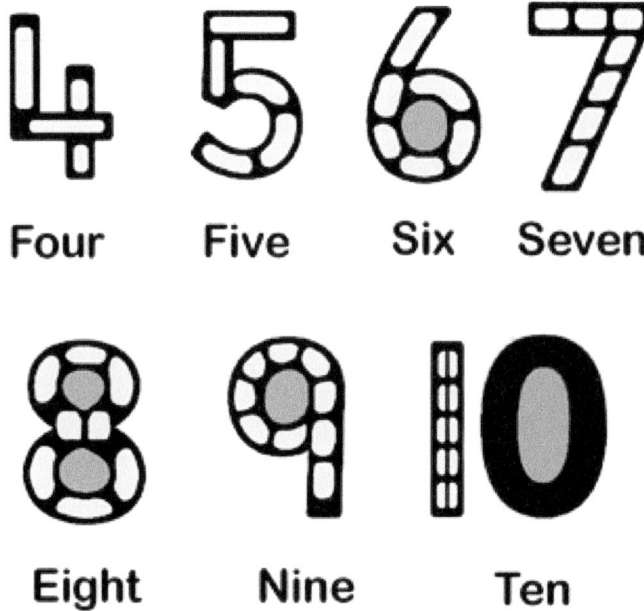

Four   Five   Six   Seven

Eight   Nine   Ten

Number Value Font

The number value font is a downloadable font for Windows and Mac that is easy to install. It comes in two formats: Number Value Font for units and Number Value Font Tens.

Number Value Font allows you to create your own sums using drawn visual associations between the symbolic shape we use to represent a number and its cardinal value. Pupils can use the spaces inside the letterform to make drawn tally marks to find the total of the sum as they count. In this version of the font, the numerals 0-9 are included.

1234567
890

Number Value Font (basic)

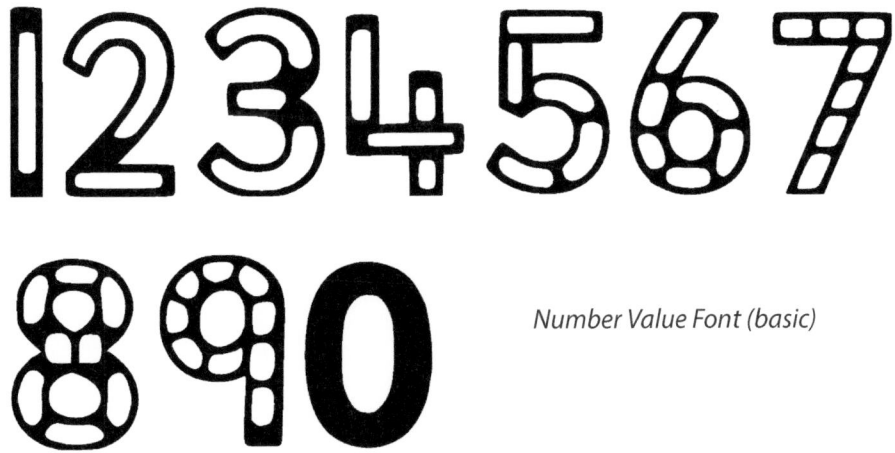

Number Value Font Tens

Number Value Font Tens represents the base numbers 1-9 in their multiples of ten equivalents. In this font, the numerical symbol for zero has been removed and replaced with a symbol for one hundred. So if you want to type a one hundred symbol, you'd need to type a zero, then when you convert it to the number font tens it will become a one hundred. This is because the zero is already included in the basic font and the value for one hundred extends the range of the font's use to 0-199. If you need to use the zero when working with number value font tens, you'd have to change back to the number value font basic.

The number value font tens allows pupils to see that the number symbol for 3 in tens equals thirty, not 3. In traditional numbers, this concept is difficult for children to learn. When counting in this font, it's easier if they just put a line through a group of fives or tens, if they can do that, because all the digits have been grouped into these values.

1234567

891

Number Value Font Tens

Using this font allows you to create your own worksheets for sums, where the digits you type contain both the symbol and the cardinal value of that symbol.

Addition

To find the product of the sum, make tally marks in each of the shapes inside the numbers, then add them all up to get the answer.

$$3 + 5 = 8$$

$$6 + 2 = 8$$

$$9 + 7 = 16$$

$$8 + 4 = 12$$

Subtraction

In the sum five minus two, two is being subtracted (taken away) from five. The number value font allows us to do that physically. We shade the two sections to be taken away from the five with a pencil, then count how many sections are left.

$$5 - 2 = 3$$

$$9 - 6 = 3$$

$$10 - 5 = 5$$

$$8 - 4 = 4$$

Division

When we divide one number by another, we are trying to find out how many times that number will 'go into' it, or in other words, how many times we can equally distribute (share) that number with the second number. For example, the number nine can be equally shared three times with three things. The number three goes into nine three times. If I had nine sweets to share between three people, they would each get three sweets. This is a difficult concept to grasp, because it requires us to hold and manipulate numbers and values in our minds to calculate the answer.

We can learn how to do this process using drawing and the number value font. For example, in the example nine divided by three, we must calculate how many times the number three will 'go into' nine. We can use coloured pens, if it is easier, to shade three sections in our number nine, and we can see this fits in easily. Then we use a second colour to shade three more sections and finally, we use a third colour to shade the last three sections. We can see it fits in exactly, with nothing left over, and we can also see we have used three colours, so the answer is three. Nine can be divided by three, three times.

$$9 \div 3 = 9 = 3$$

$$8 \div 2 = 8 = 4$$

Multiplication

When we multiply numbers, we are adding more than one amount of the same quantity. To calculate the product of any multiplication of two numbers, you can just add the same number again and again, until it matches the number of times your sum asks you for. For example, four multiplied by four is really just 4+4+4+4.

Now you can get the same answer by adding four lots of four together, but after a while, and with bigger numbers, this can become difficult. This is why we have the times tables. They are a list of the most common multiplications, but the problem with it, is that it takes a lot to remember all of them off by heart, which is what you need to be able to do, to do maths well.

The number value font enables pupils to make calculations of multiples using the slower, labour intensive, addition method. This may seem counter-intuitive, why do we want to do it the long way? Why not just try to remember the answers to the times tables? Well you can, if that's what you want and the number memory system described in this book is one way to do that.

However doing it the slower way, using drawing to make marks that represent the values of the sums, we commit it to memory better and in doing so, we understand 'why' four times four makes sixteen. We wouldn't want to consign rote learning to the dustbin, but rather use multiple methods, so that memory and understanding go hand in hand.

		4 Four	
	1		
$+ \; = $	8	2	$4 + 4 = $ 8 $2 \times 4 = $ 8
$+ \; = $	12	3	$4 + 4 + 4 = $ 12 $3 \times 4 = $ 12
$+ \; = $	16	4	$4 + 4 + 4 + 4 = 16$ $4 \times 4 = 16$
$+ \; = $	20	5	$4 + 4 + 4 + 4 + 4 = 20$ $5 \times 4 = 20$
$+ \; = $	24	6	$4 + 4 + 4 + 4 + 4 + 4 = 24$ $6 \times 4 = 24$

In this example, the four times table is set out in such a way that pupils must make drawn marks to represent the cardinal value for the number four. The number system has been set out in vertical columns to represent traditional sums. As the pupils subsequently add four more to each of the previous totals, they can see that 4+4+4+4 has the same answer as 4 x 4 and so on. Drawing with tally marks helps us to learn the times tables more effectively.

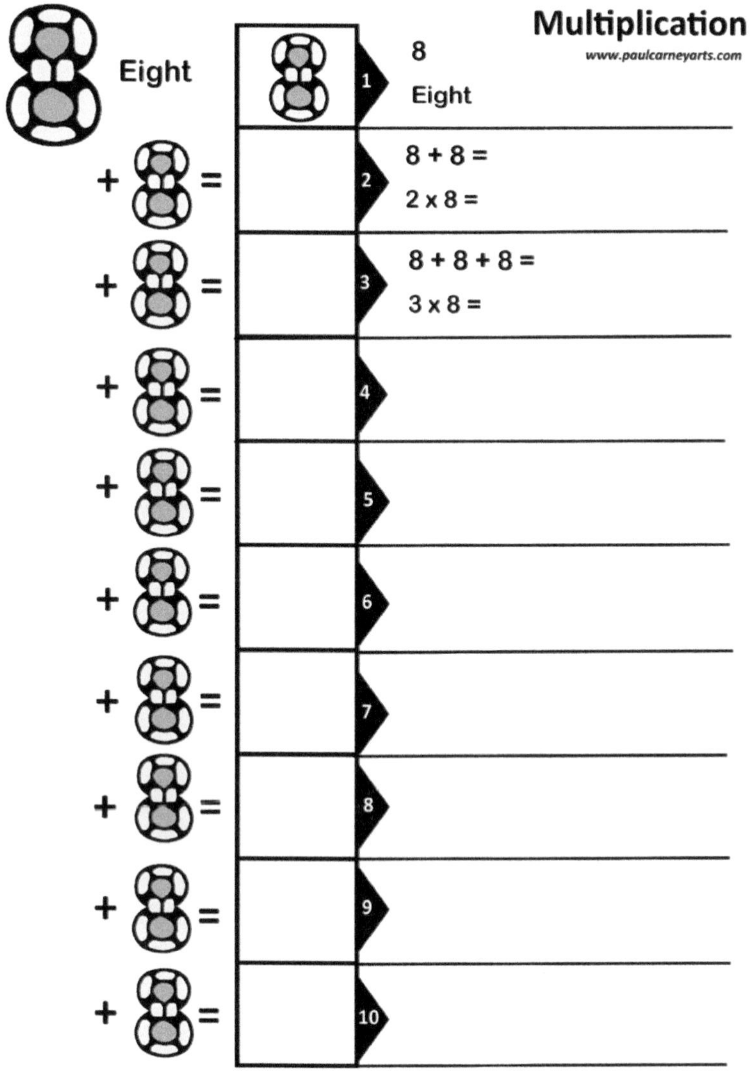

Eight

8

Eight | 1

$8 + 8 =$

$2 \times 8 =$ | 2

$8 + 8 + 8 =$

$3 \times 8 =$ | 3

| 4

| 5

| 6

| 7

| 8

| 9

| 10

Drawing operations in maths

Often, subjects require you to remember and retain sequences of information for later recall, such as operations in maths. These are hard to remember and so once again, we can use drawing to help us.

The first thing to do is to break the operation down into orderly bite size chunks. 'Do this, then do this, then look for this, etc.' Then sketch out some rough drawings to help you visualise the stages using our SSAD drawing methods.

In my example, I've produced some drawings to help me remember how to do fractions, because even at my age, I still forget what I have to do to add them or multiply them. Firstly, I made notes from a text book on what I had to do, so I understood it. Then I began my first draft stage of sketching out my ideas before I drew them up in pencil and then went over them in pen. This is what I produced:

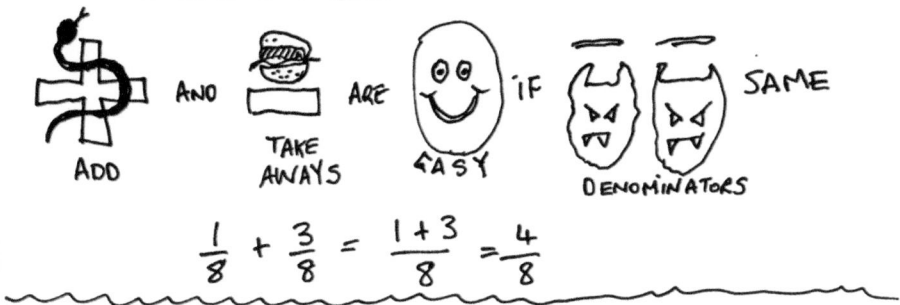

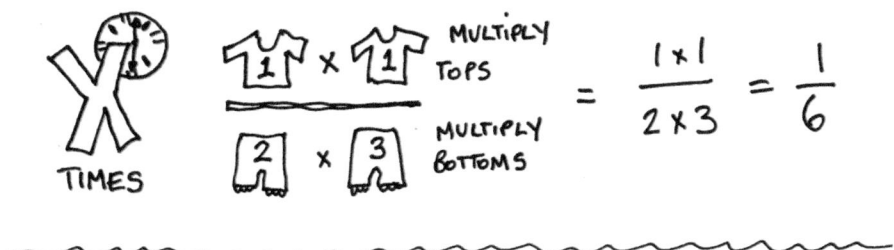

$$\frac{1}{8} + \frac{3}{8} = \frac{1+3}{8} = \frac{4}{8}$$

$$= \frac{1 \times 1}{2 \times 3} = \frac{1}{6}$$

$$\frac{1}{2} \div \frac{1}{3} = \frac{1}{2} \times \frac{3}{1} = \frac{3}{2}$$

Summary

There is a whole world of drawing in mathematics, so much so that I could have written a whole book about it. This in itself is a profound implication, because drawing can help us visualise the mathematics of the world around us and vice versa.

Iranian mathematician Maryam Mirzakhani, a personal hero of mine, constantly used drawing to elaborate her imaginative, geometric thoughts. She would draw mathematical problems for hours on huge sheets of paper laid on the floor. She is quoted as saying that she was a 'slow' problem-solver, not a quick thinker like many who are said to excel in maths, yet she was one of the greatest mathematicians of her time. Maths isn't about speed, but about understanding.

Drawing and maths aren't two separate things, they are two unique ways of describing the same phenomena. How we explore that is key to becoming better mathematicians, because as Mirzakhani said: 'I had so much fun doing it'.

$$1 \times \text{🍎 apple} + 2 \text{ 🍐🍐 pears} = £7$$
$$1 \times \text{🍎 apple} + 5 \text{ 🍐🍐🍐🍐🍐 pears} = £13$$

apple	0	1	2	3	4
pear	7	5	3	1	-1

apple	0	1	2	3	4
pear	13	8	3	-2	-7

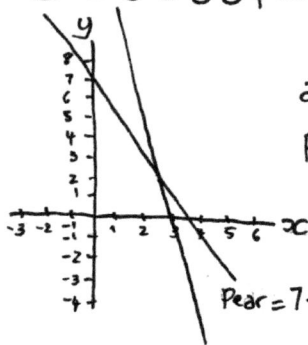

apple = £2
pear = £3

Pear = 7 − 2 apples

Pear = 13 − 5 apples

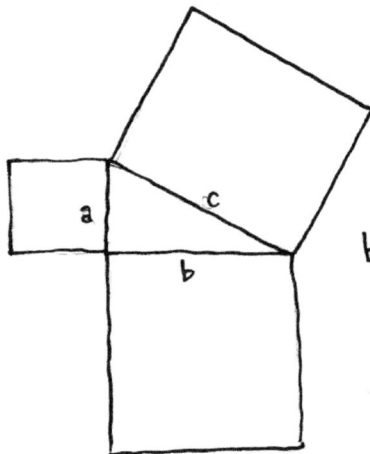

Pythagoras

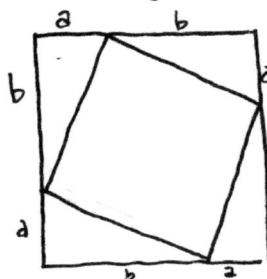

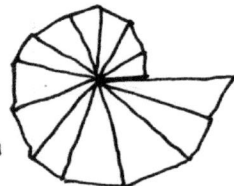

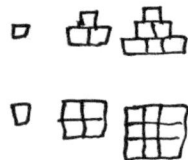

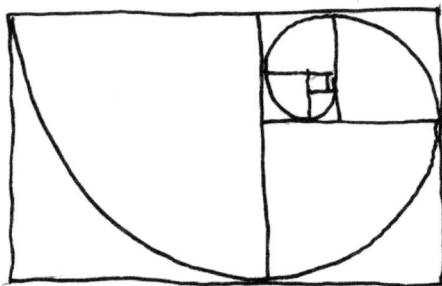

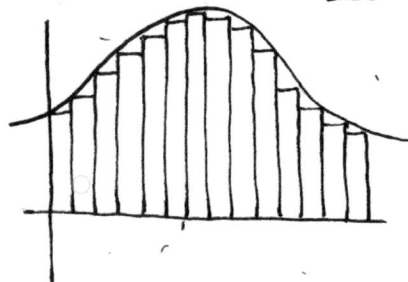

I could have filled a whole book with drawing for maths. Drawing helps us visualise and understand equations, it helps us understand harmony and balance, to draw patterns and sequences and much more. Drawing and mathematics have so much overlap because they derive from the same source.

7. DRAWING FOR INFORMATION

Drawing to observe

Outside of art and design lessons, most of the drawing you will encounter will be for information purposes rather than for aesthetic reasons. This means that the drawing should communicate information as accurately as possible, without adding any artistic, superficial details.

But why, when we can so easily take photographs, or scans or X-rays, do we need drawing at all? Surely drawing is redundant? Well I believe drawing is just as important now as it has always been. Let me demonstrate with an exercise.

Study this photograph for a minute, turn it face down, then draw what you remember.

This is my drawing. I am a trained artist with forty years professional drawing experience and I tried as hard as I could to remember the shapes of the clouds.

I've got quite a lot right with my drawing and some of the basic structure and measuring is okay, but the main cumulus cloud in the foreground is poor and not very well observed at all.

This should tell you something about our brains and how they are wired. Remember back to our memory chapter, where I described the way the brain only wants to carry the minimum amount of information it can? This is what happens when you only look at photographs. Your brain registers what it needs, then switches off. Drawing makes us slow down, take our time with the focus of our study and savour it in more detail, and it doesn't matter how good or bad the drawing is, because it is the process of observation that is important.

Photographs are very useful, but as a learning tool they have severe limitations and should be used to support observational study, not replace it. A photograph records information in its own unique way, and this is different to our eyes and minds. We can select information that is relevant for purpose and leave out what is not. We can ignore shadows if they are obscuring detail, we can read depth of field with greater clarity, understand more about the environment and behaviour of the subject and what is more, our brains connect and empathise with greater focus.

Observation drawing is a very useful tool whenever we need to study something in close detail. Scientists, botanists, geologists, architects, engineers and artists, to name but a few, are regularly required to investigate new forms by visual observation. Drawing helps us to study forms more closely, but the barrier for many people to using it is low confidence and perceived lack of skill. So many people miss out on the effectiveness of drawing because they aren't too confident of their ability.

This exercise will give you all the powerful benefits of observational drawing, for example the increased perception and awareness, but will not require any drawing skill at all. In fact, your drawing outcome will be so irrelevant you can throw it away afterwards. We do not want your attention to be absorbed by the process of drawing, nor do we want you to become agitated about the standard of your drawing. What we need is for you to focus entirely on the form you are studying through intense observation.

When we draw something, we are employing our physical, motor memory combined with our working memory. We look, we register the image in our mind, then we transfer that image through our muscle memory in our arm and hands to the paper.

A common error we make is that once the anxiety of the drawing process takes over, we stop looking as intensely. We become more focussed on our drawing than we do on studying the object. The way I used to get around this problem in my art room, was to teach blind observation drawing techniques. In this method, a piece of paper or card is placed over the drawing hand so that the artist cannot see what they are drawing. This makes the artist look more intently at the subject rather than the paper.

Blind drawing exercise

Tape a piece of drawing paper to a surface. Now puncture a hole in the centre of a second piece of paper. Place this second piece of paper over your drawing hand and push a pencil through it. Now I want you to hold your non-drawing hand in a comfortable viewing position and draw it.

However, I don't want you to draw the outside edges of your fingers or palm. I only want you to draw the inside lines, shapes, wrinkles, fingerprints, shadows and flesh. If you keep drawing the inside details you will eventually reach the edges of fingers anyway. Try to trace contours of the form and its details with your eyes. Don't skip or jump to random areas, keep a disciplined, methodical pattern, making your drawing hand follow the journey your eyes are taking. Do not be tempted to look at your drawing. I want you to really focus, to draw everything you see and not miss any detail out, however irrelevant it might seem. You should keep this drawing going for a good twenty minutes. When you are done, you might keep the drawing or discard it, it's up to you.

What I want you to do next is draw the same hand again, this time from memory. Your powers of observation will have already been greatly increased, in fact I doubt you've ever looked at your hand in so much detail, but if you want to commit it to long term recall, you'll need to draw it again from memory after an hour and then again the next day. Remember, drawing things repeatedly, with interval spacing, helps us understand and remember them so much more.

My non-skilled, blind drawing of my hand. Notice how I haven't drawn edges of fingers or the palm. By drawing only the internal details I eventually form the shape unintentionally

This technique is one that has been used by artists for generations, to help them improve their powers of observation. It isn't something to do once then forget about it, it's something to do regularly, every week if possible, with different subject matter.

Eventually you should become much more confident at drawing to record information. You should see that drawing only outside edges is not sufficient to study an object. Drawing the inner shape, the form of the thing, is vital to drawing for understanding.

It is completely irrelevant how good the final outcome of your drawing is. This is not an art lesson. You might want to keep your drawings in a journal, ink them up, decorate them or add pressed flowers, it's your choice, but to be honest mine go in the bin, because what I need is now in my head.

Conventions of information drawing

When drawing for information purposes, as either a geologist, archaeologist, architect, engineer, botanist or scientist, there are some conventions that need to be strictly adhered to if the drawing is to have an acceptable function.

- A title – stating what the focus of the drawing is.

- Time, date, direction, orientation and location – when and where was the drawing done? If outside, are there any other relevant details needed such as weather conditions, compass directions to indicate viewpoint, time of day, season etc.

- Scale – giving a clear indication of the actual size of the subject.

- Accuracy – this is not the same as being highly skilful artistically. You are aiming for precision, to record only what is there and not to invent or imagine. You should take care to ensure shapes are joined neatly, that lines meet exactly without overlapping each other.

- Organised layout – think back to the grid method I showed you in chapter one and set things out neatly. Don't clutter your drawing.

- Don't use arrows – indicate how text relates to a part of your drawing by using a single line that connects to the drawing area. Don't use arrow heads and do not allow these lines to cross over each other.

- Don't add unnecessary detail – draw only what is needed for information and leave out all decoration, embellishment and shading, unless it is important to the drawing.

Here are some do's and don'ts when drawing for information. Draw your lines cleanly and consistently. Don't leave gaps, ensure shapes are joined not open, and that lines meet correctly, not overlapping.

Do   **Don't**

Do

Draw neat, solid lines.

Join line-end junctions and shapes neatly.

Don't

Leave gaps in lines.

Leave shapes unjoined or poorly connected.

Leave joints unconnected or overlapped.

Draw arrow heads.

Drawing for information doesn't require artistic skill, but does require accuracy and precision.

Don't draw artistic representations as information drawings

Two drawings of the same geological feature. The top drawing is an artistic impression, the second is my attempt at a geological diagram. I might be wrong as I am not a geological expert, but hopefully the main differences in style and technique are obvious.

Do draw neat, diagrammatical information

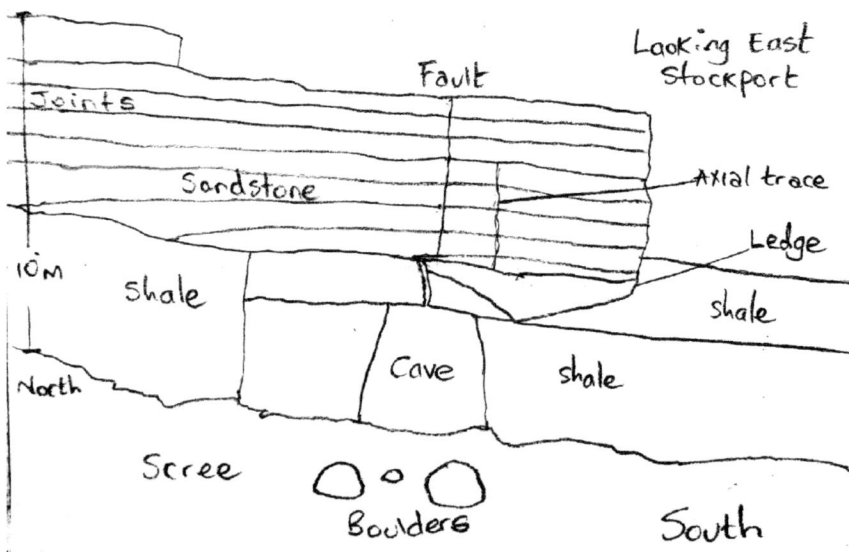

Perspective drawing

I'll just cover some basic perspective drawing now before we move on. Linear perspective drawing was developed during the Renaissance period, and is a way of representing three-dimensional solid objects on a flat surface. In this style of drawing, objects get smaller and closer together as they get further away from the observer, disappearing into a vanishing point in the distance, usually (but not always) along a horizon line.

When objects disappear into a single vanishing point it is called one-point perspective, but objects in the same picture can have several vanishing points in different places. This diagram explains it succinctly and to be honest, you'll pretty much never use any perspective more complicated than this. Copy the pictures, understand what is happening and use it when you need to.

The long lines projecting from the back of the cubes are guidelines. They are drawn to show you the angle of the edge of the cube you are drawing. You would rub them out after you have drawn them. Notice how the cube changes according to where the vanishing points are placed.

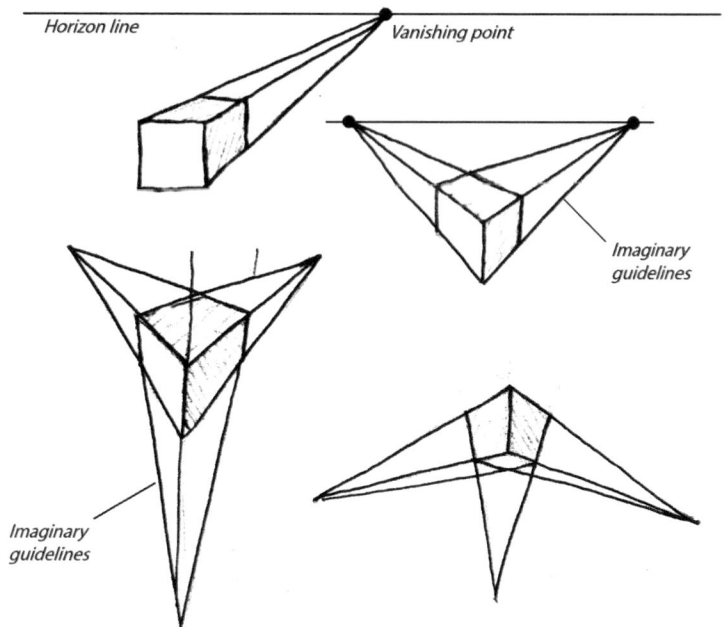

Horizon line

Vanishing point

Imaginary guidelines

Imaginary guidelines

Drawing for purpose

Drawing for informational purposes requires you to understand what it is you are drawing and why you are drawing it. You are trying to inform others what the nature of your subject is, you are directing them to features and aspects that you wish to inform others about. This requires you to understand it in the first place! If you are drawing to learn about a subject, then you are free to describe in whatever way you wish that helps you. But if you are drawing for information you should already understand it, and this means following the conventions correctly and accurately. You have to leave the artist at home and think in diagrams.

When making geological drawings the conventions state that cross-hatching or stippling cannot be used, because this detracts from, or may be confused with, geological features. However, cross-hatching or stippling can be used when drawing in biology.

Drawing in archaeology serves multiple purposes. It is used as a survey tool to produce records of sites and buildings (using a range of equipment such as GPS, GIS and 3D scanners) and to record objects for specialist publication. Also important is reconstructive illustration, to show meaningful information about past events or locations. Artists in the field of artifact illustration must work from accurate measurements of the object. Their job is to highlight information that is important to specialists, information that might not be possible to get from a photograph, such as the thickness and curves of a fragment of pottery.

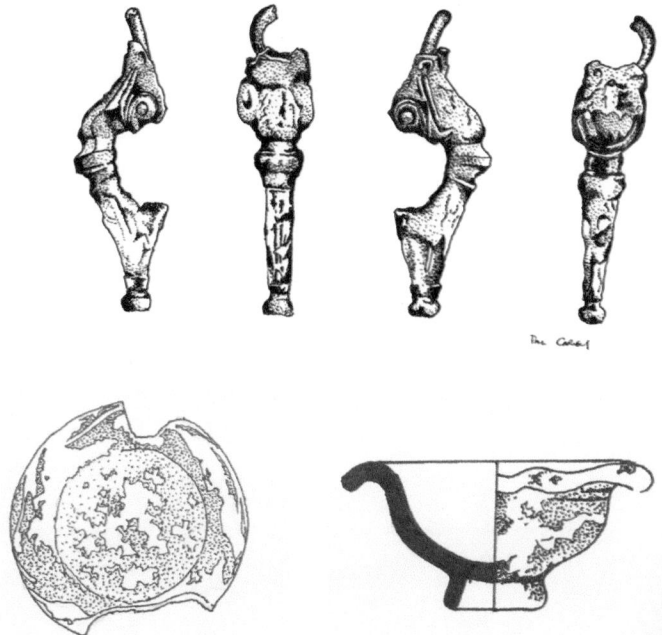

Archaeological drawings by Paul Carney of a Roman brooch and a small Roman pottery bowl. Each drawing was very carefully measured to the millimetre and rendered in black ink using stippling techniques for tonal shading. This kind of drawing provides information that cannot be conveyed through a photograph alone.

Disclaimer: I know this level of drawing is quite high, but I include it for demonstration purposes only.

Anatomical illustration has a long history and through it our understanding of human form can be mapped. For hundreds, if not thousands of years, artists and medical practitioners have used drawing to better understand the workings of our bodies. As techniques improved, such as new printing methods or new technological advancements, medical illustrations have become more and more complex, and the artists who produce them ever more knowledgeable. Anatomical illustrators must study for many years to learn their craft. Still however, the same problems of representing four-dimensional forms on a flat surface prevail through traditional drawing, and this is where digital modelling and animation can sometimes be more informative.

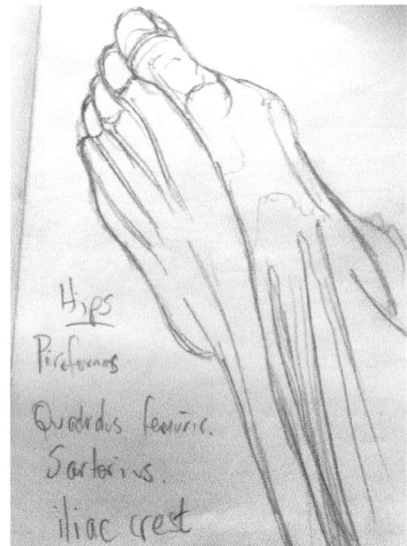

Anatomical drawings by Paul Carney of a human foot and leg produced from direct observation during a second year medical student anatomy dissection lesson. This is drawing to learn the subject, not for information.

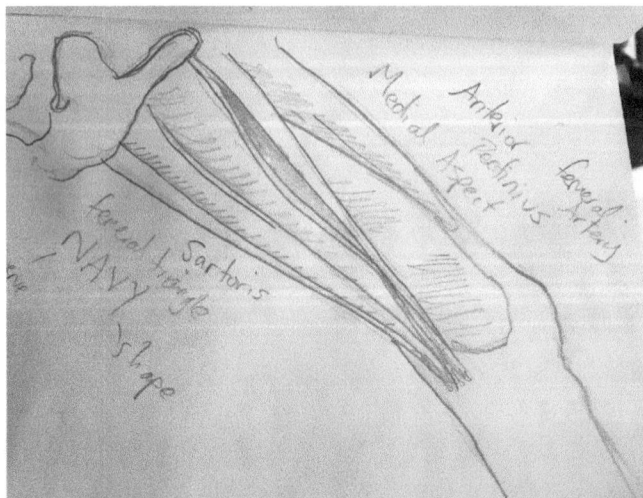

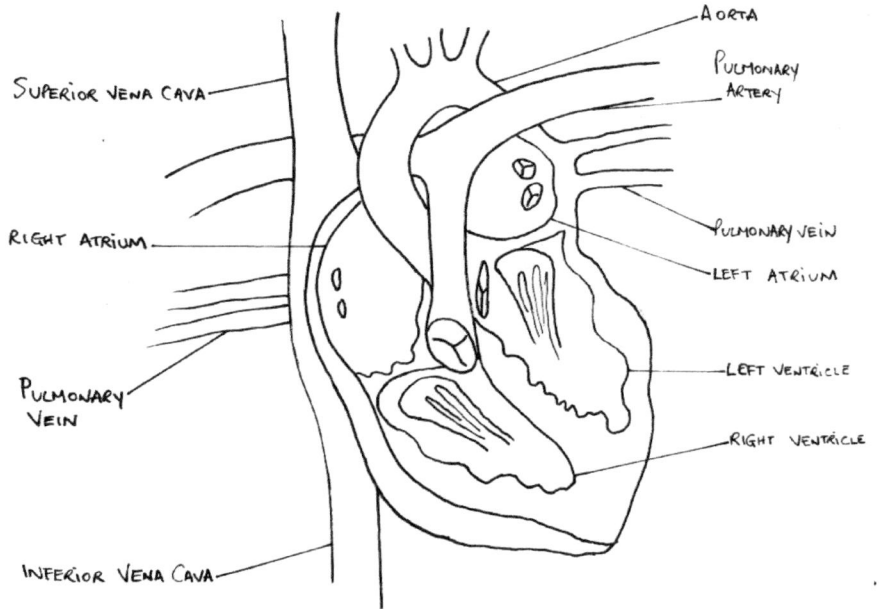

Medical diagram of the heart by Paul Carney. Note the greater accuracy, precision and neatness of the drawing following drawing for information conventions.

Labels on diagram: AORTA, PULMONARY ARTERY, SUPERIOR VENA CAVA, PULMONARY VEIN, LEFT ATRIUM, RIGHT ATRIUM, LEFT VENTRICLE, RIGHT VENTRICLE, PULMONARY VEIN, INFERIOR VENA CAVA

Again, the purpose of the drawing is paramount. Are you drawing to learn and understand the subject? If so, you are free to draw in whatever way you wish. But if you are drawing to inform others then you must follow the conventions of clarity, accuracy and precision.

Botanical illustrations are true and lifelike representations of plants. The emphasis of them is not for artistic expression, but rather for scientific information, to highlight distinguishing features. Again, close observation and accurate measurements of the specimens are important. Botanical illustrators need to have a good knowledge of biology and the morphology of the plant (its various shapes and forms) and they will work with botanical experts to ensure the correct information is displayed.

This requirement for accuracy and precision is echoed in architectural drawing where drawing is used to develop ideas and proposals for design intent of structures and buildings. Sadly, manual drawing is almost obsolete at the final presentation stage, because computer aided design is always used for greater accuracy and precision, but drawing is very much alive for initial ideas and design thinking. Here, the humble napkin has played a pivotal role in shaping many buildings, as artists sketch out ideas on them in meetings and discussions. The Shard in London designed by Italian architect Renzo Piano is one such example and the drawings of Frank Gehry are one of his major sources of inspiration.

Drawing for building construction, whilst almost entirely done on computers these days, is still extremely important. From site plans, to section and elevation drawings, structural drawings, beam layouts to electrical and plumbing drawings, drawing is the basis for all subsequent operations in the construction of every building.

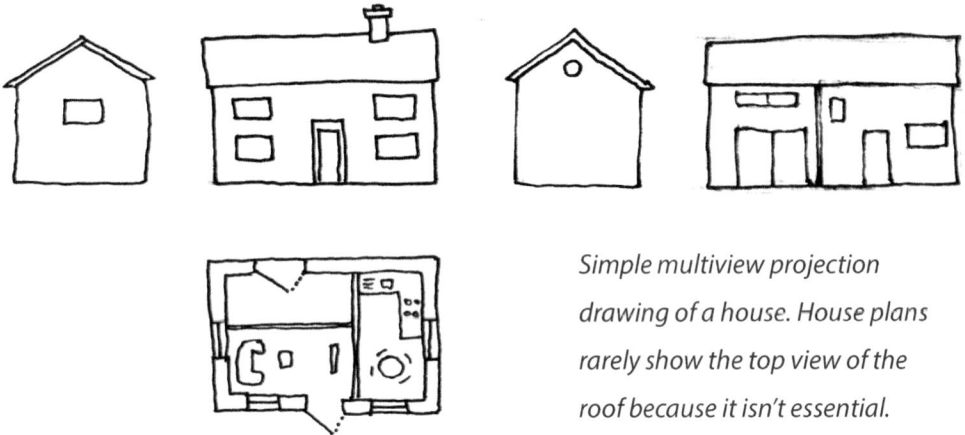

Simple multiview projection drawing of a house. House plans rarely show the top view of the roof because it isn't essential.

Multiview projection drawings are the industry standard way of representing three-dimensional objects on a flat surface. There are two formats; a European format called First-Angle Projection and a US format called Third-Angle Projection. Both formats show a three-dimensional object from all sides; top, bottom, both sides and the back, but in different orders. When drawing in this way you must follow the industry conventions I mentioned earlier regarding scale, date, measurements etc. The correct term for this drawing viewpoint is elevation. These would be front, side and rear elevations with a plan view of the building from above.

If I wanted to draw a three-dimensional drawing of my house I could draw it using Isometric Projection. This is a fancy way of asking you to draw in the style of the cube which I explained in my earlier chapter. You should be able to make out where the Y-shape would be, even though the left arm of it is missing. Other views that architects use when they draw are called cross-sections and cut-aways.

Simple isometric drawing of a house.

Cross-section drawing of a house and a cut-away drawing.

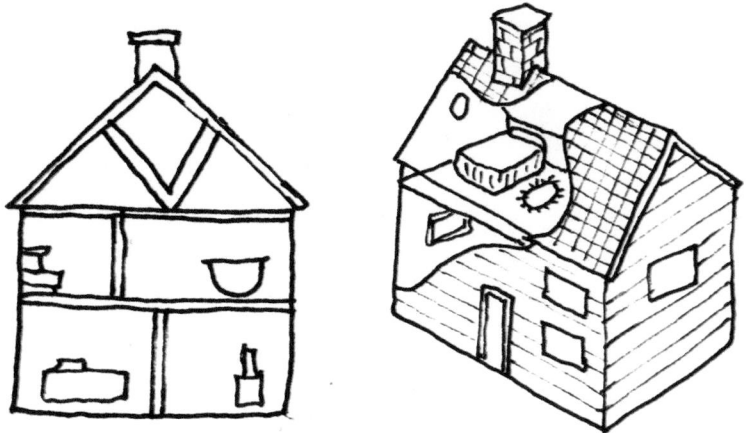

What strikes me as being really important is that, whilst the computer has become the default medium for producing accurate, precise final drawings in many areas, the initial thinking, idea and recording phase is still best done at the human level, with a pencil or pen and paper, or even with a digital pen and tablet. It is that intuitive expression from mind to paper when ideas are emerging from the brain that drawing really encapsulates, and you do not need to be an artist to draw in this way.

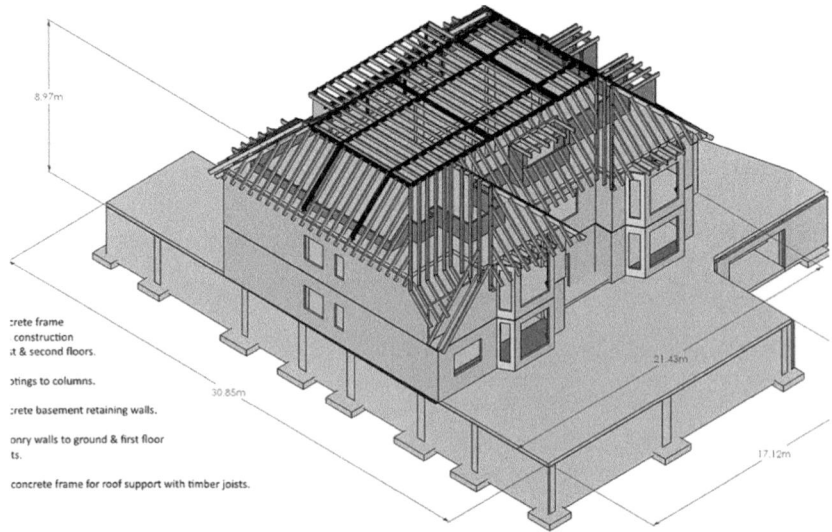

Isometric drawing of a building by Origin Structures, Richmond. Photo Steve Carney.

8.97m

:rete frame
construction
:t & second floors.

>tings to columns.

30.85m

:rete basement retaining walls.

onry walls to ground & first floor
ts.

concrete frame for roof support with timber joists.

21.43m

17.12m

Drawing diagrams compared to close observation

Diagrams are great. They simplify complex information, making it easier for us to understand and digest things that we might otherwise not understand, or forget easily. But it is important to remember that they have their limits and from what I see, they are overly used in textbooks, software and websites because of their convenience and ease of use. Remember, I said in earlier chapters that I illustrated books? I know how important it is to understand the subject of my illustration, otherwise I risk getting it wrong. That usually means researching, reading, and studying many photographs or films. It often means I have to go out and take my own photos and film if it is possible, because the process of producing a simpler version of a subject means knowing what to take out and what to leave in.

Drawing a diagram of a volcano helps you to understand some of the numerous ways volcanoes can form, but it does nothing to help you appreciate the raw energy of volcanoes erupting. Now it is unlikely that you will ever get to see that first hand, but thanks to the wonder of film and the internet, we can get to witness a good second best. So diagrams can help understanding, but only when supported by more detailed, slow observation.

You might be able to name all the medical parts of a foetus, describe the human growth cycle in detail, baffle me with medical jargon and terminology, but if you have never seen your baby in an ultrasound scan, watched a baby being born, or felt a baby kick its mother in the womb, you haven't quite understood childbirth. Both qualities are equally important. You need the technical stuff, but you also need the close, slow looking that intense observation brings, because we don't usually look at photographs that intensely, and drawing forces us to look harder.

In the first diagrammatic drawing I've copied the muscles of the forearm from a medical atlas of the human body. My source material was pretty good, a medically recommended guide used by students of anatomy. Using this, I could get a very good understanding of the superficial muscles of the arm. But I did a second drawing, this time from a gross anatomical photograph of a dissection (ugh!).

Can you see the difference? It's possible to compare some of the muscles between the two drawings, but the close observation drawing gives us a greater understanding of the complexity of the form, the mess, the incidental stuff and the imperfections. No two humans are identical and so, if we only ever see a single, stylised diagram we cannot appreciate the diversity of individuality we possess.

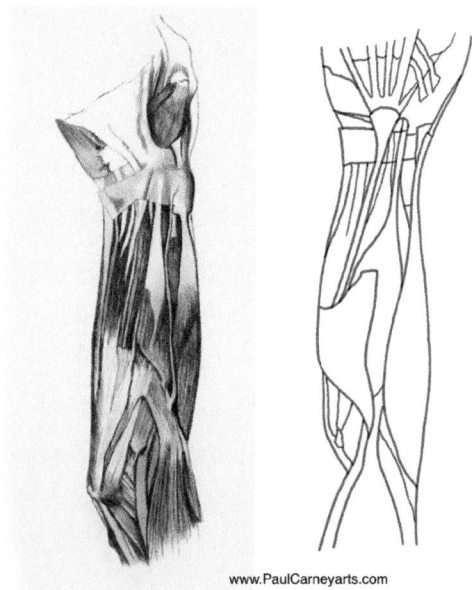

Diagrammatic drawing of the muscles of the forearm, (left) compared to close observational study from primary sources.

Regular drawing helps us to look harder and see more vividly.

www.PaulCarneyarts.com

175

My use of anatomical sources to explain my point here isn't coincidental. Doctors need to rely on their vision extensively. They have to be able to spot irregularities in human physiology quickly and correctly, even when they are unfamiliar with the patient and their body. They have to be able to tell the difference between normal irregularities in human symmetry and abnormalities.

This takes a trained eye and it is something that close observation drawing can help with. When we draw from observation, we learn to use reference points to check that we have correctly located one positional mark against another, we learn to visually check angles and measure distances between things, we learn how to describe shape and form and understand the structure of an object. Close observation drawing isn't therefore a decorative aesthetic, but the best technique we have for training people in intense, accurate seeing and recording.

But, do we need to become trained, skilled artists to benefit from close observation drawing? No, we don't!

Drawing what you don't know

There is a popular saying going around education circles right now and it is this: *'You can't think about what you don't know'*. It is used to eliminate dependency on using search engines, such as Google, to fill in gaps in our knowledge. If we don't know that we don't know something, we can hardly look it up in an encyclopaedia, can we?

But in my opinion, this binary way of approaching problem solving is flawed. We do think about what we don't know; in fact, we do it all the time. In psychology they are called 'known unknowns' or 'unknown unknowns'. Let's imagine we are trying to complete a jigsaw puzzle. If there is only one piece missing, we can speculate pretty accurately about the missing piece, its colour, pattern and shape. If there is a whole area of the jigsaw puzzle incomplete, it would be harder to speculate about the pattern and shape of the missing pieces, but not impossible. But even if we had no knowledge at all of jigsaw puzzles, then it should be possible to imagine one, with even a sparse amount of information.

This form of thinking, called speculation, is crucial to all manner of knowledge domains such as maths, science, geology, history, and art and design. We use the knowledge we have, often limited, to construct and imagine possibilities about the things we don't know. We need to be comfortable speculating about things we can't see, smell, hear, taste or touch. To use speculation successfully, you need a fair amount of visualisation. Visualisation helps us to imagine things we can't see, it helps us to construct in our minds things that are outside of our immediate knowledge.

When Dmitri Mendeleev published the periodic table of elements in 1869, he did not know all of the elements. But using the insight he had gained from his periodic table and his own speculation, he was able to predict what the then-unknown elements would be, to fill in the gaps in his table. He was, of course, using hard knowledge to ascertain what was missing. He didn't just make it up, that's not what I'm saying. We are back to our jigsaw puzzle. He had done the ground work, built up his foundations of knowledge, but sometimes, in order to complete the missing pieces of the puzzle, we have to make speculative leaps of thinking into the unknown in order to find our answers. We do this by making our known parameters clear, but then, like Mendeleev, we have to speculate, to imagine and visualise the things we don't know.

Visualising what we don't know is an all too common aspect of hard thinking, but not everyone can do it. Nor does everyone need to either. Plenty of innovators get by with limited visualisation skills, because innovation is not confined to this one discipline. However, it isn't usually taught directly. It is a by-product of some activities we do such as prediction exercises. To improve our visualisation skills, we need to practice doing visualisation exercises, so now I am going to ask you to do a visualisation drawing exercise.

Drawing a known unknown

I'll set this task on two levels: easier and harder.

Easier: 85% of the stuff our universe is made from is unknown to science. Scientists call it dark matter because they literally are in the dark about what it is. It exists all throughout the universe, it holds galaxies and planets together like an invisible glue, keeping them from flying off into chaos, yet it cannot be seen using conventional light, X-rays, ultraviolet light, radio waves or gamma rays. Some scientists think dark matter is a new form of tiny particle, others think it is the leftovers from dead stars.

So what is this mysterious substance that keeps everything in order, yet which cannot be seen? What might it look like if we could see it? Use your powers of imagination to visualise what dark matter might be, using the template provided.

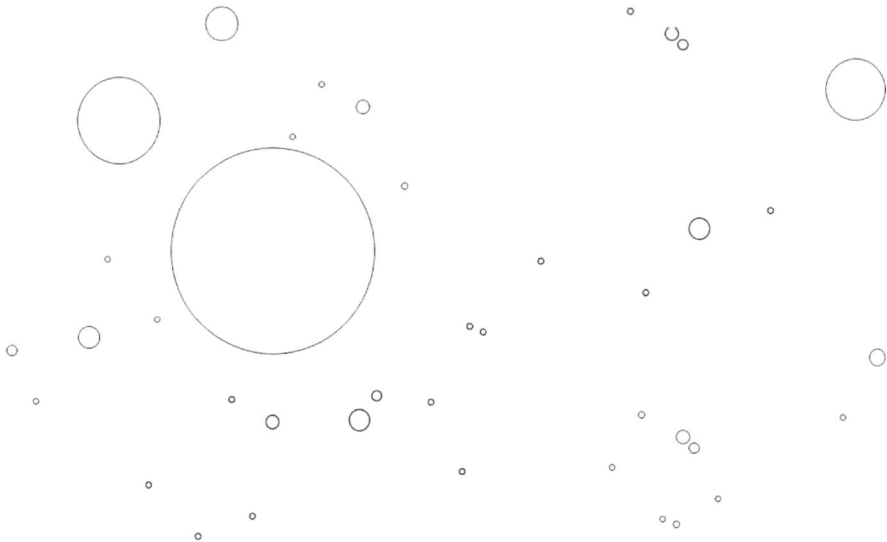

Dark matter template.

Harder: dark matter is a form of matter thought to make up 85% of the matter in the universe. Although it has never actually been seen or recorded, most scientists accept it is there because of the gravitational effects it has on the universe. Scientists looked at the amount of gas there is in between galaxies in the star clusters in space. By doing this, they discovered that there must be five times more material in the clusters than they can detect. This invisible matter is called "dark matter".

All attempts to 'see' dark matter have failed, but it has been theorised that it might be made up from collapsed or dead stars, remnants of black holes or neutron stars. Because scientists can't see dark matter directly, they have found other ways to investigate it by using gravitational lensing, which is the amount of bending light makes as it passes through matter in a galaxy.

Dark matter is classified as "cold", "warm" or "hot" according to its speed. It cannot be seen because it does not absorb, reflect or emit electromagnetic radiation (radio waves, microwaves, infrared, (visible) light, ultraviolet, X-rays, and gamma rays). But without it, the universe would descend into a wild, chaotic, free-for-all. So dark matter acts as a kind of glue that binds galaxies together. Dark matter may be a new form of sub-atomic particle or it could be a new form of matter beyond our senses.

Drawing exercise: Using the knowledge you have just been provided with, use drawing to speculate what you think dark matter might look like. Perhaps you might want to think about its molecular structure, or its general appearance. What would it look like if it cannot be seen? How does its 'appearance' change as its velocity changes? Would it have a texture or feel to it? What smell or taste might it have? Do you think it resembles a cloud of gas, or is it more tangible like glue? Does it float in space or wrap itself around interstellar objects? Clearly, dark matter must be huge if it makes up 85% of the matter in the universe.

Drawing our emotions

Whilst we can see the effects of emotions on people's faces, in their body language or expressions, emotions themselves cannot be seen.

What are emotions? Where do they exist? Where do they come from? What shape and form do they take? Do all emotions look the same? Are they an electrical or chemical signal, or are they more robust and three-dimensional, like a protein shape? How do they move between areas of our brain and body? Where are they going to and what do they do once they get there? So many questions need answering.

You might want to research emotional signals in the body, or to find out what neural pathways look like. Emotions must be exceedingly small, whatever form they take.

Once you have found out as much information as you can about the known science of emotional signals, I'd like you to try to draw or paint what you think they might look like in our brains and bodies.

Are the molecules or signals responsible for producing fear the same shape, colour and texture as the ones that make us happy? Depict not only the molecule or signal, but the environment it lives in, using your research to help you.

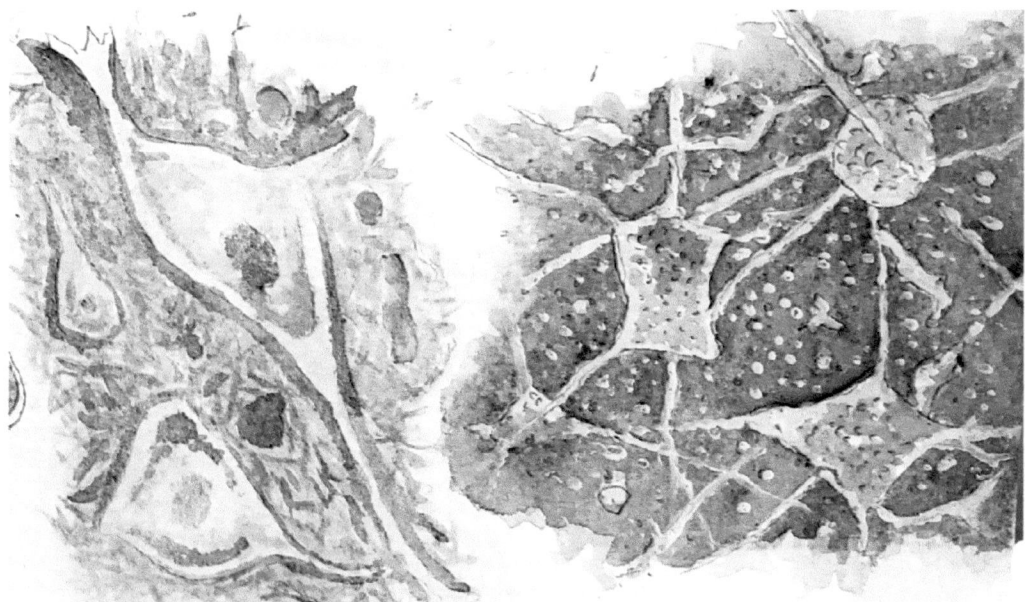

Emotions

You might take a wild, imaginative and humorous approach, by inventing characters for each emotion we feel. You might take a pattern based approach, thinking of the shapes of molecules and how they interlock with each other. Perhaps you might look at other molecules to get ideas, such as proteins which have a vast array of wonderful, complex shapes. You might think in an abstract way, or use digital technology, or even think of ideas using clay or wire.

In this exercise, you will be making a tiny, almost imperceptible world big!

Drawing exercises like this are extremely challenging because there are so few frames of reference. But if you think about it, it also means you can't be wrong!

SUMMARY

I began this book by saying 'if you can say it, you can draw it. If you can write it, you can draw it.'

Drawing isn't only a decorative, bolt-on feature to be added to an essay to make it look good. It isn't only a front cover, an insert, a graph or a chart. It is a form of thinking. It is the most effective way to remember stuff. It helps us to get our thoughts out of our heads. This isn't a trivial process. It is as important as writing. It is communication.

We don't need to be able to draw like an artist. We don't need high technical skill, to be a Leonardo da Vinci or a Salvador Dali. We need to get over our embarrassment, to become so familiar with our drawings that we don't even think about the level of skill we are producing.

Children and teachers should be drawing every day as part of learning. Exercise books shouldn't be free of graffiti, but full of appropriate, relevant graffiti related to what we are learning. Humans have drawn for hundreds of thousands of years. Our intellectual development can be measured by it, it is inherent in our cognition.

Students think nothing of writing reams and reams of information that they promptly forget. Drawing might just be a pleasurable antidote to this and transform you into a successful learner.

REFERENCES

Myra A. Fernandes, Jeffrey D. Wammes, and Melissa E. Meade (2018), *The Surprisingly Powerful Influence of Drawing on Memory*, Department of Psychology, University of Waterloo. Available at: http://www.hsredesign.org/wp-content/uploads/2019/04/Impact-of-drawing-on-memory.pdf (accessed February 2021)

I was influenced by a blog page written by Doug Lemov on Close Reading, which I used to focus my drawings and illustrate meaning for a passage from the book To Kill a Mockingbird by Harper Lee. Blog available at: https://teachlikeachampion.com/blog/close-reading-preview-establishing-meaning/ (accessed February 2021)

The science experiment in Drawing in Four Dimensions was adapted from an inertia experiment on Steve Spangler's science website. Permissions given by Steve Spangler. Original available at: https://www.stevespanglerscience.com/lab/experiments/inertia-ring/ (accessed February 2021)

Supporting images for structural engineering provided by Steve Carney, Origin Structures, Richmond, N Yorks. https://www.originstructures.co.uk/

AUTHOR PROFILE

Paul Carney is a nationally recognised, National Society for Education in Art and Design (NSEAD) registered, art consultant having delivered specialist art Continuing Professional Development in schools, colleges, galleries and universities across the UK and for the UK's leading training providers. Paul is a fellow of the Royal Society of the Arts, specialises in teaching drawing and painting and is a practicing professional artist and designer. He is a former Council member for the NSEAD, which means he is involved in national art education issues.

Paul lives in Newcastle upon Tyne where he runs his highly successful art website: paulcarneyarts.com which provides high quality teaching resources and advice to teachers around the world. He has over twenty years teaching experience at Primary, Secondary and Post-16 levels of education, is an Advanced Skills Teacher, an ex-Subject Leader for Art & Design and was a member of the NSEAD Curriculum Writing Group that wrote the art curriculum competencies, more formally called the: 'Framework for Progression, Planning for Learning, Assessment, Recording and Reporting 2014.'

BV - #0117 - 030621 - C0 - 246/189/11 - PB - 9781909671249 - Matt Lamination